MESSAGES OF HOPE

Preaching Peace and Justice for All

SHEILA HARVEY

WESTBOW
PRESS®
A DIVISION OF THOMAS NELSON
& ZONDERVAN

WestBow Press books may be ordered through booksellers or by contacting:

WestBow Press
A Division of Thomas Nelson & Zondervan
1663 Liberty Drive
Bloomington, IN 47403
www.westbowpress.com
844-714-3454

Scripture taken from the King James Version of the Bible.

ISBN: 978-1-6642-6285-0 (sc)
ISBN: 978-1-6642-6287-4 (hc)
ISBN: 978-1-6642-6286-7 (e)

Library of Congress Control Number: 2022906289

Print information available on the last page.

WestBow Press rev. date: 04/22/2022

To my colleagues who support me
on the journey towards peace and justice for all –
the congregations who have called me to serve as their clergy, and to
my beloved Union, as their first African-American, and
first woman full-time pastor.

To my extended family and God-sent, confidants
traveling with me through the years.

To my loved ones who choose to support me the most;
my mother Linda, sister Sharon, son Brandon, and BFF Charles –
you all fill my cup daily.

To God Be the Glory for the Promise of Peace and Justice for All!
*Let there be peace and justice throughout the land,
known on every mountain and hill. Psalm 72:3, ERV*

CONTENTS

CHAPTER 1   THE EASTER SEASON

Letter 1   Christ Is Risen 1

Why is it still important to tell others that Christ lives?

Letter 2   Holy Language 7

In what ways does the holy language of peace still speak today?

Letter 3   Breaking Bread 11

How might we respond to Jesus' invitation to break bread with Him?

Letter 4   Powerful Witness 17

How might our lives be powerful witnesses for Christ?

Letter 5   Enduring Witness 23

How might we live as an enduring witness for Christ?

Letter 6   Witness of Love 29

How does God's Spirit offer us a witness of love?

Letter 7   Spirit of Welcome 35

How might we welcome all people who feel like outsiders?

CHAPTER 2   THE SEASON OF PENTECOST

Letter 8   Pentecost Sunday... 43

What does Pentecost Sunday mean in our lives today?

Letter 9   This is Good.. 49

Are we willing to accept God's invitation to love all creation?

Letter 10 Sacrifice... 55

What sacrificial work are we being called to carry out?

Letter 11 Daring Disciples... 61

In what ways should we dare to put God first in our daily lives?

Letter 12 Holy Welcome... 67

How can we show a holy welcome towards all people?

Letter 13 Chosen Journeys... 73

How might we open our hearts to love others courageously?

Letter 14 Wheat and Weeds Together................................ 79

How does God want us all to live together?

Letter 15 Weaving the Future... 85

How can God's love weave into the hearts of believers today?

Letter 16 Face to Face.. 91

In what ways do we experience being face to face with God?

Letter 17 When All Seems Lost.. 97

How can we hold on to hope in those times when all seems lost?

Letter 18 Bold Moves..103

How can we make bold moves toward the plan God has for us?

Letter 19 Be Transformed... 109

What does it take to be transformed by God's love?

Letter 20 Spirit-led Living... 115

How might God's Spirit lead us to harmonious living?

Letter 21 Remember, Restore, Renew..............................121

How might remembering God's faithfulness restore and renew us today?

Letter 22 Road to Freedom 127

Are we willing to be on the road to freedom?

Letter 23 Tension in the Wilderness............................... 133

How can we face tension and stress in the wilderness moments of life?

Letter 24 God's Sustaining Presence 139

How might God's presence sustain our lives?

Letter 25 Wisdom for the Way..145

What is God's wisdom calling upon us to do?

Letter 26 Praiseworthy Living.. 151

What does it mean for us to offer praiseworthy living?

Letter 27 Living Messages...157

How can our faith reveal that God's mercy still exists among us today?

Letter 28 The Compassionate Life 163

How might God's vision of compassionate living give us hope?

Letter 29 Partners in Service..169

How might we act as equal partners in Godly service?

Letter 30 Tending God's Light..175

How can we keep our light shining for God?

Letter 31 Extravagant Opportunity 181

How might we boldly use our gifts and talents to please God?

Letter 32 Reigning Compassion 187

*What challenges prevent us from
responding in love to the most vulnerable?*

CHAPTER 3   THE SEASON OF ADVENT

Letter 33 Where are You, God?..195

How do we wait with hope for something greater to come?

Letter 34 A Hope for Peace 201

How can our actions reinforce Christ's perfect peace?

Letter 35 Shouts of Joy... 207

How might we find joy, even during times of pain?

Letter 36 Birthing a Promise 213

What does the promised birth of Jesus Christ mean for us today?

Letter 37 Christmas Eve Reflection 219

CHAPTER 4   THE CHRISTMAS AND EPIPHANY SEASONS

Letter 38 Long-Awaited Gift... 227

What does the long-awaited gift of Christ's birth mean for us today?

Letter 39 Epiphany Celebration.. 233

How might we celebrate Christ's light in the New Year?

Letter 40 Defining Moments.. 239

*How might the defining moments of
Christ's baptism offer us a fresh start?*

Letter 41 Known and Loved 245

How might God's role in our lives impact others?

Letter 42 Follow Me 251

In what ways is God calling us to move into a new future?

Letter 43 Power to Do 257

*How might we allow the power of God's
love to cleanse our hearts and minds?*

Letter 44 Source of Strength.. 263

In what ways can God be the healing source of strength for us today?

Letter 45 Compassionate Community............................... 267

How might we experience the glory of God today?

CHAPTER 5   THE LENTEN SEASON

Letter 46 God's Loving Paths 277

What does it mean to trust in God?

Letter 47 Always Close 283

How might we respond to God's faithfulness today?

Letter 48 Beautiful Law 289

How might we live according to God's beautiful law?

Letter 49 No Matter What 295

How do we see God's love at work today?

Letter 50 Deep in Our Hearts... 301

How do we keep our hearts filled with Godly love?

Letter 51 Into Jerusalem 307

What does it mean to celebrate Jesus?

Letter 52 It's Time to Exhale...313

The Conclusion..317

Letter 53 Now What? 319

Endnotes 325

CHAPTER ONE

THE EASTER SEASON

Leading up to the Easter Season of 2020, news about COVID-19 becoming a threat to American lives dominated the headlines. In January, COVID's first-known case in the U.S., by way of a Washington State man who had traveled from the city of Wuhan in China. Americans living in Wuhan were evacuated and tested in a California airbase. Efforts began to isolate all with the COVID-19 virus. In February, national news focused on the impeachment of former President Trump by the House. Later, the charges of abuse of power and obstruction of Congress were determined not guilty by the Senate. But, in March, the focus of the national news was back on COVID-19. The World Health Organization declared COVID-19 a global pandemic, and the 2020 Olympics could not happen as scheduled. "The CBS Evening News" also reports COVID-19 may infect up to 70% of the world's population. [1] In addition, hospitals began discussing how best to prepare for the impacts of COVID-19. Trump also admits to Bob Woodward that he downplayed the COVID-19 threat in the early days of the outbreak.

April saw tension. On April 30, 2020, militia group members pose in front of the Governor's office after protesters occupied the State Capitol during a vote to approve the extension of Governor Gretchen Whitmer's emergency coronavirus declaration/stay-at-home order in Lansing, Michigan. Reuters reported later in October that federal and state authorities charged 13 people for plots to kidnap the Democratic Governor. Several governors ask for White House help in calling off militant protestors, and "The CBS Evening News" reports anti-vaxxers were spreading fear about the COVID-19 vaccine. In May, the world responds in anger over the cruel death of George Floyd. This heartless act sparked protests in favor of justice and equality worldwide. Police officers kneel in solidarity with protesters in several U.S. cities. And, the top prosecutor in St. Louis says, "good police officers "can't sit in complicit silence" when it comes to racial justice.[2]

PRAYER

Faithful God, you conquered death and opened the gates of life everlasting. In the power of the Holy Spirit, raise us so we may also proclaim resurrection hope, and love towards one another. Amen.

LETTER ONE

Christ Is Risen

Why is it still important to tell others that Christ lives?

<u>Sunday, April 12, 2020</u>
<u>Easter/Resurrection Sunday</u>

Christ Is Risen
On this Easter Sunday, we can almost hear the voice of Mary Magdalene shouting to all who would listen, 'He's **Alive. Hallelujah, Jesus is Alive!'**

And so, the question for us today is, **"Why is it still important to tell others that Christ lives?"**

We can <u>first believe that Christ's Resurrection reminds us to remain hopeful in all things</u> so that we will <u>secondly; be a witness to God's transformative love for us all.</u>

Let us imagine, for a moment, what it must have felt like being Mary Magdalene on that Easter Sunday, seeing two angels sitting in the empty tomb then, seeing Jesus once more and speaking to Him.

At first, Mary Magdalene was so overcome with grief that she did not initially recognize Jesus, but glory filled her heart and soul when He called her by name. Then, hopelessness turned into joy as joy, turned into gladness, and she said to Him, with all the love in her heart Master, YOU are alive!

This resurrection message reminds me of an old seminary story about believing in God, which calls upon us to embrace Mary's encounter with Jesus by encouraging us to experience God for ourselves.

The story takes place during a seminary lecture debunking the Resurrection when a visiting preacher responded by showing everyone that faith is like tasting an apple, it is personal, and the crowd applauded. [3]

As the 34th Psalm says, "O taste and see that the LORD is good; [and] blessed is the [one] who trusts in Him (Psalm 34:8, KJV) for, it will change your whole life, forever.

Now, let us return to our question, **"Why is it still important to tell others that Christ lives?"**

The scripture teaches that everyone needs to experience a personal relationship with God, especially in uncertainty, grief, and loss. Because when we have a personal relationship with God, we can bear witness that even when it seems that all hope is gone, God's love will help us to rise and face the challenges ahead. And that is why the psalm reading for today tells us that even when the evidence points to us being pounded down, we are still lifted!! And for this, we should rejoice because God is more extensive, more creative, and more grace-filled than we are.

As we are to believe that whatever the day brings, God is with us, God will take care of us, and that God will see us through it.

Being transformed is exampled in the famous story about a millionaire who visited a sixth-grade class in East Harlem. And because they were facing statistics that stated most of them would drop out of high school before graduation, he decided to do something that could change their lives.[4]

He decided to speak from his heart during his visit and told them to 'Stay in school.' Then, he went on to say, 'that if you do, I will help pay the college tuition for every one of you.'

And at that moment, the lives of many of these students changed, as one student put it. 'Now, I have something to look forward to; I have something waiting for me. And that is a glorious feeling.'

The follow-up to this story is that nearly 90 percent of those 59 students graduated from high school!!

And that is why we hear of God's transformative love told today by Jeremiah, who tells us that the Israelites were able to find hope, even in their wilderness season.

Jesus Christ arose for the lonely, the bereaved, the parent who lost a child, the elderly couple seeing life slip away.

Christ arose for those who are unemployed. He emerged for those in estranged relationships/ Christ appeared for those searching for life's meaning.

Christ arose to bring the light of hope when it seems we are in our bleakest hour. As

Hope motivates when it seems discouragement comes.
Hope energizes when the body seems tired.
Hope sweetens while bitterness seems to bite.
Hope sings when it seems all melodies are gone.
Hope believes when the evidence seems eliminated.
Hope listens for answers when no one seems to be talking.
Hope climbs over obstacles when it seems no one is helping.
Hope endures hardship when it seems no one is caring.
Hope smiles confidently when it seems no one is laughing.
Hope reaches for answers when no one seems to be asking.
Hope presses toward victory when no one seems to be encouraging.
Hope dares to give when it seems no one is sharing, and

Hope brings the victory when no one seems to be winning.
(John Maxwell from Think on These Things)

It is the kind of hope that God shows us when Jesus hung, bled, and died on the cross and was placed in the tomb on that Friday evening with the plan that three days later, Jesus Christ would rise again and come out of that tomb!

It is why we hope against all hope because it is the most significant relationship anyone could ever have, for we know that God's love does not leave us. God's love does not grow old, nor will it ever lose its value. Love is the fullness of who God is. And we know this because 1John 4:8, NIV, tells us that "God is love." We are never more like God than when we love like God. And we are never closer to God than when we allow God's love into our hearts. "For God so loved the world that he gave his only, begotten Son, that whosoever believeth in him, should not perish, but have everlasting, life." [5]

So, on this Easter Sunday, let us share Christ's light by bearing witness to the relationship that we have with God. Let us invite all to taste and see God's transformative hope and love. And let us be like Mary, crying out in joy because our Lord and Savior, Jesus Christ, lives, and His light guides us still. May it be so. **AMEN.**

PRAYER

Gracious God, your love reaches us through fear and doubt; your love reaches us through wounds and scars. Help us to hear your words of peace and healing; fill our hearts with joy so that we may continue to confess you as our God. Amen.

LETTER TWO

Holy Language

In what ways does the holy language of peace still speak today?

Sunday, April 19, 2020
Second Sunday of Easter

Holy Language
This second Sunday of Easter builds upon the Good News that Christ is Risen! As we hear the Holy Language of Jesus offering words of peace and healing to the disciples during their difficult circumstances.

And as we journey together during this Easter Season, our question becomes, **"In what ways does the holy language of peace still speak today?"**

We can first explore God's peace in our fears so that we can secondly; believe that God's presence is always with us, even in our doubts.

In today's scripture, we see that the early disciples struggled with their faith because they witnessed the crucifixion and thought their lives were in danger for being followers of Jesus. And because of this, they hid behind locked doors in fear. These early believers are not so different from how many of us feel right now. Because like those disciples, we also are huddled behind locked doors for our safety, praying for God to help us in these uncertain times.

7

As their faith was shaken but, it was not dead as suddenly, on that first Easter evening, while they huddled together terrified in that locked room, everything changed. And amid all their worry and anxiety, the risen Savior came back into their lives.

And His first words were, "Peace be with you," [6] which is what they most needed to hear. They needed their lives, their thoughts, their hopes, and their dreams back again. They needed to be set free from the fear that locked away their faith. They required that only Christ give them peace, forgiveness, new hope, and a reason for living.

This message is also illustrated in a story about an artist commissioned to depict peace. But, after failed attempts, the artist felt led to finally paint a stormy nighttime sea with a bird nestled in the rocks. And, this painting was accepted.

Like the painting depicting peace, Jesus came to the disciples while they were dealing with the stormy seas of doubt and riding on the waves of hope, saying, "Peace be with you." [7]

Jesus offers the holy language of peace to the disciples who hid away in that locked building and helped them overcome their fears so that they might live in perfect peace.

Bringing us back to our question, **"In what ways does the holy language of peace still speak today?"**

As we might say, God is still speaking to us to be making us whole again by restoring us to the goodness that God has created in us.

But, when misfortune and hardship come our way, it can be challenging to trust in God's promises. Yet, when we are huddled inside of a place amid storms whirling all around us, whether we are lying in a hospital bed or living with grief or depression depleting our faith, God says, "Fear not!" [8]

We can try and hide from all the difficulties of this world, but Christ will find us there. But, more than anything else, when Jesus appears to the disciples behind closed doors, he is showing them, unmistakably, that there were no doors that could keep Him out. There was no way the disciples could be separated from Christ. And that there was no circumstance in which they would ever be alone. And this is the good news that God brings to each of us each day.

There is no closed door that can keep the love of God away from us. And there is no locked door that can shut us apart from God. There is no viral pandemic nor storm-ravaged corner of our lives that is too powerful for God as God will provide us with what we need to overcome it.

That is why we hear today's Psalm reading bear witness to the joy found by being in the powerful presence of God. In that, we cannot live our lives without experiencing times of great fear and anxiety. But, despite all the hurt and harm the world can and does inflict upon us, God's compassion and care are with us, still.

This message of faith reminds us that there are times when we realize there is a power far greater than our own. And this reality is exampled by stories told of several survivors of tornado storms who lived to tell their stories.

Many of us can only imagine the anxiety of those moments of being completely powerless and knowing that our loved one was out there somewhere in great danger. And yet, all we could do was wait for the rescue crews to come to help. [9] These stories are yet, another example of what Christ does for us as Christ offers hope amid life's fears and uncertainties.

That is why we can trust that there is hope for each of us in all our anxieties. We can trust that there is help when we feel like giving up. And we can trust that faith will help us overcome our fears because there is One who can enter any room. There is One who can overcome any problem. There is One who can bring peace to every anxious heart. Because, on this day and every day, Jesus Christ is the One who reaches out his healing hands to us and shows us his wounded side saying, "Peace be with you." [10] So, then, let us trust that God's Word of peace speaks to the loving power that will never leave us alone. **Amen.**

PRAYER

Ever-present God open our eyes and hearts to recognize Jesus in our lives, and in each other. May we live in and share the light of the Resurrection, knowing that we journey with and towards you. **Amen.**

LETTER THREE

Breaking Bread

How might we respond to Jesus' invitation to break bread with Him?

Sunday, April 26, 2020
Third Sunday of Easter

Breaking Bread
This third Sunday of Easter continues to build upon the Good News that Christ is Risen! We learn about Jesus breaking bread with the two disciples whose restored faith saw that He lives!

And in our journey together during this Easter Season, we may ask, **"How might we respond to Jesus's invitation to break bread with Him?"**

Jesus teaches us first to open our hearts to God's grace so that we can secondly extend our loving grace towards one another.

In our story for today, two of Jesus' disciples were walking toward a small village called Emmaus, and along their walk, they witnessed everything that happened to Jesus and were now going back home, discouraged and without hope. [11]

Yet, amid their hopelessness, Jesus shows up and appears in a way that they do not expect. But, He is making Himself known in their hearts.

A great example of God's presence in our hearts is shared about a heart surgeon who could not understand the kind of faith that gives hope to a sick child. [12]

The story takes place in a hospital with a surgeon who just performed open-heart surgery on a child who told him he would 'find Jesus in her heart.' And, a divine, calming presence appears after he concludes the child only had months left to live.

Later, the surgeon met with the child and her parents. When the child opened her eyes and asked, "What did you find in my heart?" In tears, he says, "I found Jesus there."

Now, let us return to our question, **"How might we respond to Jesus's invitation to break bread with Him?"**

We can respond to Jesus' invitation by loving deeply from within our hearts. In that, Jesus is the bread of life broken for us, to strengthen our faith and restore our hope in God. As Jesus speaks to our hearts, and in doing so reminds us of God's abiding love.

Because, like the disciples, we may not always see that the things we need most are right here, among us. But, in those times, when we are so preoccupied with our concerns or griefs, we do not realize that God is among us. In that, we may spend years refusing to recognize God and start believing that we are on the road of our own, making.

And as a result, we can become blind to or even ignore the presence of God. But, when we look back, we see like the disciples on the way to Emmaus that God's presence is with us every step of the way.

And therefore, we hear in the reading of Acts about the importance of baptism that speaks to the forgiving grace of God, not just for a nation or a race of people but God's grace, which is available for us all.

The psalmist we heard today gives a great example of accepting the invitation to break bread with God and moving from suffering and distress to giving thanks for life and witnessing to others about what God has done.

But, like the psalmist, many bear witness to God's transforming love. This kind of transformation is found in the story of Cinderella. She begins as a mistreated step-sister and later becomes the belle of the Ball.

It is the kind of transformation found in the story of Aladdin, who starts as a petty thief and later becomes the Prince.

It is like the transformation that we see in the story of David, who began as the little shepherd boy and later, in the blink of an eye, stood victorious over standing the Giant.

It is the transformation of a woman, who began namelessly, and later became known as the Mary, who poured expensive perfume on Jesus' head and is remembered for her beautiful act toward the Lord.

It is the story of a despised tax collector, looked down upon by everyone in society, who later entertained the Savior in his own home.

We all can give witness to the transforming love of God because Jesus invites everyone to break bread at the table of God's grace!

This story about the two disciples walking toward Emmaus reminds us that while we may lose hope and question our faith, God still has a plan for our lives.

And that is why the songwriter says that "I am leaning on the everlasting arms of Jesus" [13] because when we are feeling broken, and it seems that life is unfair, we can rest in knowing that Jesus is with us, and not just part of the way but, even in our weariness Jesus, will carry us all of the way even into glory!!!

When we lean on the everlasting arms of Jesus, we open our hearts and hands to trust that by faith, all things are possible through Jesus Christ, whose living bread strengthens you and, who strengthens, me.

And so, as we embrace God's countless blessings that surround us, may we also continue to allow the divine love that is always with us and within us to flow through us to be a blessing, not only towards ourselves but towards others, as well. Breaking bread reminds us that Jesus Christ is in our hearts with every morning that has broken. And yet, He is resurrected so that we can live with the hope that feeds our souls with the Good News message, which teaches us that no matter what we are going through, God is with us, and *it will all be, okay*! May it be so. **Amen.**

PRAYER

Loving God, we know you as being like a Shepherd, a Friend, and even more to us. Help us recognize your generosity and all-embracing love so that we may also be generous and compassionate towards others.
Amen.

LETTER FOUR

Powerful Witness

How might our lives be powerful witnesses for Christ?

<u>Sunday, May 3, 2020</u>
<u>Fourth Sunday of Easter</u>

Powerful Witness
On this Good Shepherd Sunday, we are reminded that God's shepherding comes to restore our lives. As we hear the powerful witness about Jesus as the Good Shepherd who leads us, comforts us, renews us, and shows us how to care for one another along the journey.

And in hearing this, we may ask, **"How might our lives be a powerful witness for Christ today?"**

<u>The scriptures suggest that we first open our lives to God's leading so that we, secondly, experience and testify to God's love.</u>

Let us, for a moment, imagine the image of Jesus as being the Good Shepherd in the ways that we care for one another. Because when we do, Jesus looks like you, and He looks like me, helping us all to understand better why the scriptures teach us that we are all created in the image of God.

There is an excellent story about the divine connection of enormous redwood trees in California! Some are 300 feet high with an intertwined root system to help sustain each other. So, when the storms come, they remain standing. What a powerful witness to the glory of God. [14]

And like those redwood trees, the early Christians mentioned in the book of Acts is an example of the kind of powerful witness, of a community gathered together, by God's love.

Bringing us back to our question, **"How might our lives serve as a powerful witness for Christ today?"**

As we can live, trusting that no matter what happens in our lives, 'our cup runneth over,' [15] because we are all part of God's beloved community created equally, as powerful witnesses to God's abundant love!!

And that is why we, like the writer of the 23rd Psalm, can boldly proclaim the ways that God is our shepherd in that God WILL supply our needs and PROMISES to lead us down the right paths.

Our need for a Good Shepherd is in the story of Tabitha. It speaks of a lovely woman named Tabitha who was busy doing good work in her town. But, she had become ill and eventually passed away. So, when the people heard that Peter, who was known to represent Christ, was just down the road, they sent for him. And, when Peter heard the news, he made the twelve-mile walk to the town of Joppa and found the house where Tabitha's body was lying at rest.

And so, when Peter arrives, the widows who loved Tabitha took him upstairs, where their friends' body was at rest. Then something beautiful happened. The ladies took out the robes and other articles of clothing that Tabitha made while reminiscing with one another as they mourned her death.

We can imagine that Tabitha's friends spoke of how she had touched their lives and the poor people of their city with the articles of clothing she had made. It seems Tabitha had touched people's lives because of her commitment to Jesus and her ability to make clothing. But God was not finished with her yet; God was going to breathe life back into Tabitha's spirit. And when Peter says, "Get up," the breath of life enters Tabitha, and she arises. [16]

And while they did not have the kind of social media we have today. Tabitha's friends seem to have had their way of socializing because it was not long before everybody knew that Peter, like Jesus, was granted by the power of God to raise Tabitha from the dead. And because of this, all who heard about what happened also believed in the resurrecting power of Jesus Christ.

As God will raise us from whatever is troubling us. Even when it seems like all the life in our situation is gone. And our hopes for any future have been dashed.

There are seasons of life that lead us through deep valleys, and it seems that the sun will never shine again. Because, if we live long enough, there will be days when it looks like the walls of life are caving in, all around us, and, as hard as we try to hold up those walls, we cannot seem to do it alone as the hard times can drain us. The hard times can exhaust us. The hard times can take away the enthusiasm and excitement of life.

And yet, while we could try to convince ourselves that these hard times are something new and that life is unfair, the truth is that hard times are nothing new, and in fact, hard times come in many different packages. Sometimes they wrap themselves in a hospital gown at an ICU unit. At other times, they manifest in a marriage gone wrong, a child gone astray, or a job ending with no prospects.

Hard times can be seen as physical limitations, mental constraints being emotionally fragile, or even experiencing the loss of hope. Any of these things happening in our lives can lead us to experience hard times.

And these were the kind of hard times that the people who loved Tabitha experienced as they fell upon hard times when she passed away because she helped so many. And their hope had been replaced with hopelessness.

Hard times had taken their toll, but God was not finished with them yet. Tabitha rose again, was given new life, and became a powerful witness to God's glory.

As being risen again, with new life was also what happened among those early Christians, who gathered together in community to serve the common good and to respond, as best as they could, towards one another's needs. In that, the church's witness of the early church is a testimony about how they lived together, even during hard times!

Like the early church, we also witness the power of Jesus Christ in our lives on an ongoing basis! In that, a powerful witness is through our prayers. We share the joys and life's hardships as our powerful witness is in our singing hymns and songs of praise. Powerful witness occurs when we break bread in honor of the salvation of Christ. And powerful witness happens when we come together to study the Word of God, and hear the Word of God, to better understand our faith.

This powerful witness helps us minister Christ's love in the community by offering love to God and one another through acts of mercy, justice, and kindness. And in doing so, some of us minister by showing up and helping with our food pantry on Saturdays. There is so much effort that goes into helping our neighbors to have food to eat. Many help to minister in this way. We serve as good shepherds in the community on behalf of those who need something to eat.

Some of us minister by offering leadership in the life of the church. There are so many things needed to help sustain Christ's church. But, because so many in our church family are willing to serve on our ministry teams, we can offer meaningful worship, fellowship, Sunday School classes for our children, along with our various mission and outreach ministries. And we can only do these things because we have a good and loving shepherd, in Jesus Christ, who examples for us the importance of serving with a glad and generous heart.

And so, let our powerful witness be rooted in the guidance of our Lord and Savior, Jesus Christ. Let Christ's teaching guide us, renew our lives, and raise us from our valleys. And let us remember daily that by our faith, **all things are possible through Christ, who strengthens us** to emulate God's love, hope, and compassion along our life's journey. May it be so. **Amen.**

PRAYER

Life-giving God breathe upon us your Spirit of new life like that of a life-giving and caring Mother. Help us recognize your generosity and all-embracing love so that we might also be live-giving and compassionate towards others. **Amen.**

LETTER FIVE

Enduring Witness

How might we live as an enduring witness for Christ?

Sunday, May 10, 2020
Fifth Sunday of Easter (Mother's Day)

Enduring Witness
On this Mother's Day Sunday, we continue in the Easter Season, building upon the Good News that Christ is Risen. Jesus encourages the disciples to be an **enduring witness** of God's love by telling them that a place is ready for them in God's eternal realm.

And in hearing this, we may ask, **"How might we live as an enduring witness... for Christ?"**

The scripture suggests that we first learn to trust in God's faithful and steadfast love so that we, secondly, more fully commit ourselves to be God's love in our living.

In reflecting on how we might fully commit ourselves to the enduring witness of God's love, we can look to a biblical story about two mothers as the story begins with Eunice. She had a baby boy named Timothy. And when the boy was still young, Eunice's dad died, so they asked her mother, Lois, to come and live with them. [17] As it is said, that little Timmy was a delight to everyone.

23

As we understand that both his mother and grandmother spent countless hours with him, teaching him the stories of the Old Testament, praying with him and for him, and training him in the things of God. And while they did not have an iPhone, internet access, or even cable television, they created a spiritual environment right where they lived so that little Timmy could flourish.

Then, one day, a preacher named Paul came to their town of Lystra and spoke about a man named Jesus. And when Paul said, Lois and Eunice listened intently. And the more they heard, it had become clear to them that Jesus came as the fulfillment of all the promises told in the Old Testament. As a result, they decided to trust Jesus Christ and were converted and afterward began to focus on teaching Timothy all about Jesus.

These mothers saw the enduring witness of God through Paul teaching them about Jesus. And because of their commitment to being God's love in the way they lived, the Bible tells us that Timothy, himself, later served as a witness of God's love by continuing to spread the Good News of Jesus Christ throughout the area!

As this story exampled for us, the importance of community shows us the importance of being connected as a family of believers connecting as believers who understand that we need each other spiritually and that God has a purpose for us all.

Now, let us now return to our question, **"How might we live as an enduring witness for Christ?"**

Our enduring witness can be like Eunice and Lois in those times, when we live with the life-giving love of a caring mother figure whose love for God, love for oneself, and love for others become living examples, of the all-embracing love, of Jesus Christ.

As we see the enduring witness of God's steadfast love also exampled in today's reading of Psalm 31:3, NIV when we hear of God being our rock, who leads us. The psalmist shares that God is our rock who guides us, and God is our rock who saves us. Therefore, God is our refuge in times of suffering and is with us whenever we are in need.

Another example of being an enduring witness for God is in Acts. A man, by the name of Stephen is called to go boldly and tell the mighty acts of Christ. As Stephen is, going and being a witness for Jesus Christ by telling everyone who would listen that God's love is so great that He sent His Son, Jesus, to save us all.

And as Stephen's message of Jesus Christ spread, it began to threaten those in power, and as a result, Stephen's punishment was death.

But, in those moments, Stephen discovers that he has significant opposition, and it seems like he is all alone. Yet, Stephen still finds peace even amid dying an unjust death. Stephen's faith in a loving God far surpasses the evil that is causing those in opposition to throw stones at him. Stephen believes that Jesus Christ is his living stone and is with him even in what seems to be the worst of times.

As the scriptures prove, this is so by telling us while Stephen is dying, he gazes into heaven and sees Christ reigning in glory.

Today, the Good News is that we, too, are surrounded by God's love through Jesus Christ, who tells us that there are preparations for us but that all we need to do is trust Him in all things.

This Good News reminds us that no matter what, Jesus is the solid rock to build our faith. And because of this promise, we can trust that more extraordinary things are on the horizon as Jesus Christ promises to be with us, and that is why He tells the disciples that He will send the Holy Spirit to guard and guide us all forever.

Like each of us, by our faith, are the living stones of Jesus Christ. We embrace a united and uniting church in the Word of God. We welcome the call upon us all to love one another as God loves us. We are a church with a courageous faith that seeks to embody the message of Jesus Christ as the 'good teacher.' [18] This message calls upon us to be enduring witnesses against the 'evil teachings' of bigotry that promote inequalities based upon gender, race, class, sexual orientation, nationality, disability, or anything else, that separates us from loving all of God's, children. We proclaim to be the Church of Jesus Christ, the One who lives. We might know more fully of God's all-embracing love that is equally amongst us all.

As Jesus is the way, through our hard times, He is the way, through our grief. Jesus is the way, through parenting, and Jesus, is the way, towards home. Because He is the way, to everlasting glory!!

And so, as we continuously seek to 'live the Jesus way,' let us strive to be like Eunice and her mother. Let us do so by embracing God's love and sharing it with our loved ones as they did with Timothy so that by our witness, there will be many others who become great witnesses for Christ!

And let us also seek to be like Stephen, who seeks to remain firm in our faith by trusting that God is with us continuously until death.

And in doing so, let us seek an enduring witness for God's love. Let us do so, trusting that our faith in God will spread from the inside of our being, spilling over into Sunday morning worship permeating throughout our Zoom videoconference calls and overflowing into the lives of our families, friends, and neighbors near and far. We are trusting that because Jesus Christ is our living stone. He is also our solid rock, upon which we all can stand. So, no matter what we are going through, we can rest assured that our lives are purpose-filled and that each of our lives has meaning. And, even when we stumble, God's faithfulness, and steadfast love, forgive us and give us new life like that of a life-giving and caring mother!!

For Christ is Risen so that we might be re-birthed, in God's Spirit, with the fullness of life trusting in what Jesus said and believing, there is a place that has already been prepared for us far beyond this life, as we know it. Because none of us will make it out of this place, physically alive. The Good News is that God's glory awaits us in heaven. Let it be so, for us all, O God. **Amen, and Amen.**

PRAYER

Loving God of us all, thank you for your spirit of truth that unites us. Thank you in that your presence with us is constant. Unite us as one body to support and strengthen one another.
Amen.

LETTER SIX

Witness of Love

How does God's Spirit offer us a witness of love?

<u>Sunday, May 17, 2020</u>
<u>Sixth Sunday of Easter</u>

Witness of Love

This Sunday, we continue in the Easter Season with the Good News that Christ is Risen. As we learn in today's scripture Jesus breaks the news to the disciples that He will leave them but also assures them that the Holy Spirit, the spirit of truth, will come and serve as God's **witness of love** - to be their comforter always!

And so, we might ask, **"How does God's Spirit offer us a witness of love today?"**

<u>As the scripture suggests, first, no matter what happens- God's Spirit is present with us- offering help, comfort, and courage, which helps us to secondly, be able to unite as one body in Christ- so that we may support and strengthen one another.</u>

It is important to note that when Jesus is speaking to the disciples, they are in an upper room and having the Last Supper with Jesus. This passage is relevant because we are only a couple of weeks away from Pentecost, the time when the Spirit comes to the disciples, just as Jesus promised it would once He departed from them.

And so, in preparation for His departure from the disciples, Jesus promises that the Holy Spirit will come to be their advocate. Jesus also promises the Holy Spirit will be a comforter who will help and guide them, especially in their time of need. Jesus further shares that the Holy Spirit will come alive in them by living out the two greatest commandments; loving God and loving one another!

Jesus encourages the disciples to remain faithful even though they are fearful and uncertain of the days ahead so that they can be comforted and encouraged that God will not leave them alone in their time of need.

This scripture suggests that Jesus is indeed witnessing to the disciples about God's love for them! Proclaiming as the One who knows what is - and what is to come, revealing the presence of God's Spirit in the world, and sharing the incredible love that God has for everyone!

Godly love is the kind of all-encompassing love that was revealed here at Union during our Spirit-led advocacy of Justice and Peace in educational worship moments. It travels experiences, which allow us to hear witnesses of God's love for us and our neighbors through the life and ministry of Jesus' call for humanity to rise above those things that seek to divide us and seek instead to offer acts of love amongst, one another!

Godly love is the kind of all-inclusive love at the core principles of our wider church, the United Church of Christ. Our bold and brave stance on the love God has for all of humanity is the kind of love that embraces all people from all places. The sort of open-hearted love offers an extravagant welcome into this sacred space, which is God's household of faith!

As witnessing to God's love is what Jesus teaches us what it means to be a true friend by our sharing and being the love of God towards one another, especially in our times of need. And that is why the old hymn. What a friend we have in Jesus is a timeless classic. Because a good friend is hard to find, think about it. How often have we been disappointed by the lack of support? Or how often have we failed to measure up to the expectations of being a good friend?

Jesus speaks about the importance of having a friend because we all need one another. We have been created in a community, not in isolation. In that, there will be times when it feels like we are walking through fire, carrying heavy burdens and doing so by ourselves.

Jesus teaches that when we worship God, rather than the human desires and comforts of this world, we will suffer with, and for the sake, which inherently is a lonely experience.

Even though our faith may lead us to feel abandoned, our insistence on love and justice can put us at odds with the world, and even with those closest to us, we still have the assurance through the Spirit of God that we will always have a friend, in Jesus.

Bringing us back to our question, **"How does God's Spirit offer us a witness of love today?"**

We can respond by being a witness to God's Spirit of love in our lives and in the ways that we show Godly love towards one another.

And like Jesus, our witness of God's love among one another, reminds us of the comfort and strength that the Spirit of truth offers for us all! Because, regardless of what is going on in our lives, Jesus teaches us there is more to come!

There is more in store for us, more than we know to ask for, more than the eye can see, and, more than we can hope for, or even imagine! And, all that we are to do is show love.

There is a legendary story about Agatha, an 87-year old, who would cook daily for people in need. [19] When asked, 'Why?' She replied, "because *I love it.*"

Sheila Harvey

There are many Agatha's here at Union, too! We do so by showing our love towards one another. In that, we witness the light and love of Christ that lives in our hearts—in turn, shining right back out into the world! What a wonderful kind of love! The everlasting love of Jesus Christ! Love that never abandons us! Love that is with us always!

Now, that is a story worth telling. The story of love. A love that never lets us go. A love that allows us to choose to accept love or embrace it. Our choosing love will enable us to know that we are never alone nor, are we ever, abandoned by God.

And so, let us continue embracing the loving Spirit of God, to see that we are all loved equally by God. In that, we are all created in the image of God and are called good. Let us also remain witnesses of God's love by being united and uniting in Christ so that we can continue to be the true love that Jesus Christ has called us to be, for ourselves, and in the world! **Amen.**

PRAYER

God of us all, we thank you for your Spirit that unites us. Thank you, in that your presence with us is constant. Unite us as one body to support and strengthen one another. **Amen.**

LETTER SEVEN

Spirit of Welcome

How might we welcome all people who feel like outsiders?

Sunday, May 24, 2020
Seventh Sunday of Easter

Spirit of Witness
On this Sunday, where we recognize our fallen heroes who defended our nation, we learn in today's scripture that Paul boldly supports the loving message of Jesus Christ, who saves all and has no boundaries. As Paul shares with the church in Galatia that through Christ, there are no outsiders, and all are welcome to become part of the family of faith.

And so, we might ask, **"How might we welcome someone who feels like an outsider into our family of faith?"**

The scripture suggests that we are to first hold on to our belief in God in our daily living so that we can, secondly, model the goodness of God for others.

It is important to note that Paul was Christianity's greatest missionary and truly believed that all are welcome into the family of faith. And because of this belief, he established churches all along the Eastern Mediterranean, Turkey, and Greece as Paul preached a gospel of God's love and grace through the life, death, and Resurrection of Jesus Christ.

Paul stressed that nothing a person can do to earn God's love—it was God's gift to us- because no one is perfect.

And so, in Paul's preaching, there was no altar call. There was no demand that people pray a "sinner's prayer," confessing their sins and accepting Jesus Christ as their Lord and Savior. Being filled with the Holy Spirit and speaking in tongues was not expected. And, it didn't take two verifiable miracles to make you a saint.

As Paul shared, life in God's kingdom was ultimately a gift. And that a person received this gift by faith. That faith believes that Jesus has risen from the dead and trusts that God moves in believers' lives and the world. But, simply sharing God's grace and love wasn't enough for the believers in Galatia. They wanted there to be something more required before welcoming the non-Christians into their family of faith.

As the Jewish Christians believed to earn God's favor, outsiders must prove that they were faithful by being circumcised, eating Kosher, and observing the Sabbath. And accomplishing these tasks would give them the satisfaction and the security that they had done something worthy of the relationship with God they wanted. But, it was the exact opposite of what Paul preached.

There are two perspectives. If we look at ourselves and concentrate on what we have done and what we believe, it is then when we are focusing on work and earning God's acceptance. Yet, we look to God and are overwhelmed by God's love, grace, and presence in our lives. Both perspectives allow us to know what Paul wants the Galatians and other Christians to experience. He suggests that we regularly offer a gracious welcome for ourselves and others into the family of faith, no matter where we all are along the journey.

Bringing us back to our question, **"How might we welcome someone who feels like an outsider into our family of faith?"**

As we can respond by simply continue believing that the presence of God is among us in our own lives so that we can be a model for living out our faith by showing God's goodness for others when they come our way.

Paul reminds the early Christians of how Jesus modeled love for us. The gospel message is a message of New Life-Now! To be lived out on this side of eternity. Friends, Jesus never leaves us the way he found us.

Jesus gives us a new heart. He sends the Holy Spirit to live within us, empowering us to live a life filled with an overflowing of what we need.

Jesus fills us with an overflowing of his peace and with his joy. A life that continually transforms us into the image of Jesus' love so that we will not conform to this world. But instead, be full of joy and allow the passion of God's love to flow within us and from us.

For example, suppose you wanted to learn to dance. And you go to a bookstore and buy a book on dancing. Take the book home, and you get started.

You continue to read, then dance, read, then dance until the end. Then, you plop exhausted on the couch, look at your loved one, and with great pride, say that you executed it perfectly. Then your loved one acknowledges your accomplishment but says that you forgot the essential part - the music!

You didn't think about music. You just focused on learning the rules. You laid out the pattern. But you forgot the music. And so, your sweetheart goes on to suggest that you do it again and then put in a CD. Instead of worrying about the steps, you follow the music this time. And the next thing you know, you are following the music while dancing with your partner.

Because when we allow God's love to move us, transform us, and guide us, we can truly love ourselves and one another within our hearts. And we can begin to hear music unlike we have never heard it so that our feet can learn to dance like never before.

By moving together and showing our love towards one another, we embrace the love of Christ. We are the love of Christ. We are witnessing the light and the love of Christ that lives in our hearts and, in turn, shines right back into the world! What a wonderful kind of love! The everlasting love of Jesus Christ! Love that never abandons us! Love that is with us always!

And as we honor our fallen heroes, I think of those who serve our nation with such strong faith alongside people from various walks of life but who come together for a common purpose. And in doing some research on how those who serve care for each other, I read about a term called 'battle buddies,' which is a system that states no one is ever to be alone in the battle.

You can't even go to the bathroom alone as the idea is that we need each other. I need your faith, and you need mine.

There is a story about a promise kept from a 'battle buddy' who delivered personal mementos to his sister, Grace, upon his death. When Grace received the memento, she was relieved. [20]

This story reminds us not to give up on our faith by finding the strength to hold on to what God has in store for our lives and the lives of others.

In that, our faith will transform us into welcoming an outsider and help us have a willing and loving heart to serve God so that we can love ourselves and then be able to offer love towards one another.

And in our doing so, let us continue to embrace the loving Spirit of God in our lives, and as a church, let us also remain in Christ as one body, united and uniting as a family of faith. And let us continue to be the love that Jesus Christ has called us to be for ourselves and in the world! **Amen.**

CHAPTER TWO

THE SEASON OF PENTECOST

Pentecost would come towards the end of May. Efforts of peaceful protesting continued. In June, peaceful protesters near the White House faced a forcible order to move out of the way to allow President Trump to pose outside a church holding a Bible. A reverend says she was among those tear-gassed so that Trump could "hold a Bible and look Christian." [21] Former President Trump also says he is the "president of law and order" and declares aggressive action on violent protests.

Juggling the need to remain safely distanced and the desire to keep the economy going, on July 23, the Major Baseball League returned on opening day at Dodger Stadium in Los Angeles. There was an audience of cardboard cut-outs of people placed in the stadium, but many MBL players opted out. In August, news reports show devastation in our nation, as Hurricane Laura flooded buildings and homes on the Louisiana Gulf Coast. And, the summer ends with the nation mourning the death of U.S. Supreme Justice Ruth Bader Ginsburg. Judge Amy Coney Barrett filled Ginsburg's seat.

In October, the coronavirus enters the White House. Former President Trump was diagnosed with COVID-19, hospitalized, and released. News headlines reported that at least 25 people close to the former president also tested positive for COVID-19. During this time, the former president did not encourage mask-wearing. Top doctors re-emphasized the importance of wearing a mask for protection against the coronavirus. On November 3, the nation voted, and on November 7, Joe Biden was named the projected winner of the 2020 presidential election. Former President Trump disagreed with the outcome and sought to overturn the courts' results and some state legislatures. Georgia leaders reject Trump's push to overturn the election results; the Supreme Court rejects Texas's request to overturn the election in four states. The Supreme Court rejects the GOP request to overturn election results in Pennsylvania.

PRAYER

Loving Creator, blow your Spirit upon us, send it to challenge and comfort us. Let it be the lifeblood that pulses through our veins so that we might be made whole and new. Amen.

LETTER EIGHT

Pentecost Sunday

What does Pentecost Sunday mean in our lives today?

Sunday, May 31, 2020
Pentecost Sunday

PENTECOST SUNDAY

Here we are on this Pentecost Sunday! Pentecost celebrates the time when the Spirit came for all people and changed the lives of thousands in just one day! Pentecost celebrates that memorable day of Pentecost when the believers experienced the Spirit of God!

And in hearing this, we might ask, **"What does Pentecost Sunday mean in our lives today?"**

As the scripture first suggests, when God's Spirit fills our hearts, we can be renewed with the love of Christ so that we might secondly be made whole and new.

Let us reflect on those believers who gathered in the upper room to pray on that day.

Pentecost occurred ten days after Jesus Christ ascended to heaven and fifty days after the Resurrection. And the believers needed once again to experience the presence of God. And so, while they were praying, they were hoping. Hoping that in some way, they could be renewed in their faith in God, hoping that they could in some way restore their relationship with God and to have a sense of peace.

And it was so! As the Spirit came powerfully and mysteriously - coming to fulfill the promise of Jesus Christ, who shared with the believers just before He left that God would send the Holy Spirit to be present with them. As it was in this moment of Pentecost that the church began. It was at this moment when God's Spirit would renew all. In this moment of restoration, it was when to go out with excitement and spread the Good News that all might receive salvation by being baptized through God's Holy Spirit!

Now, this was Good News for these believers! And because of this, the people left that upper room and began sharing this message. Resulting in thousands of people being becoming Christians with their lives forever changed!

As the scripture teaches, God meets us, right where we are restoring and renewing us during our times of need.

An example of God being with us is in a story titled, 'The Master's Hand," about a child slipping away to the stage, plucking, "Twinkle, Twinkle Little Star." But, when the master pianist played alongside the child, the concerned audience became mesmerized.

As it seems, this was the feeling, at Pentecost when the Holy Spirit's presence was at work, reminding the believers they were not alone and that together with God, they will be the people to transform the world and, to even, mesmerize it.

Now, let us go back to the question, **"What does Pentecost Sunday mean in our lives today?"**

As our passage suggests that Pentecost Sunday examples for us that we are to keep praying so that we experience God's Spirit, meeting us right where we are!!

Along our journey, there may be times that cause us to be like those early Christians: going into our upper rooms to pray and praying that God hears our cries. Praying that God comes in a mighty and powerful way to help restore our faith. And as we face today's injustices and solutions toward a peaceful way forward, we continue to remain prayerful for the presence of God's power and the Holy Spirit to strengthen us as we need strength to continue onward in our faithful living and witness for a better tomorrow.

But, what does it mean to be a faithful witness, especially in times like these when people are clearly, angry over the racism that remains after so many years of working towards racial justice. What does it mean to be a faithful witness in these times when it seems like the cries for justice for blacks' lives to matter are met with resistance from white supremacists? What does that mean for my little black boy and the other black boys growing up in America today? What does Jesus say about all who stand in opposition to racism, or any injustice, for that matter?

And yet, the answer to these questions is clear. Jesus sends the Holy Spirit to light a fire from within to strengthen and courage us to go out from our prayer rooms and tell about the fire of justice birthed on Pentecost Sunday. This Spirit-fire calls upon us to go out and be the light of Christ in the world by educating and witnessing to others in our words and deeds that we are all loved and created equally by our ever-present God.

And so, let us do what those early Christians did on that first Pentecost Sunday, and go out into the world spreading the Good News that the presence of God is with us always. Let us go out into the world advocating for a more just world for the sake of peace.

We go out into the world shining the light of Christ by lifting our lights high for all to see that we have been created equally in God's love. And therefore, seek ways to live together, united, as one human race.

As for myself, I find it exciting to go out and tell others about the ways that God's Spirit is blessing this church. And when faced with the common question of how things are going at the church, I say things are great. I say that things are great because I cannot help but think of the many ways that God's Spirit is upon this church!

God has blessed us with a kind of love beyond what a person looks like or a person's background! And when we share in our welcome, whether in-person or online week after week, by saying, 'No matter who you are, or where you are on life's journey, you are welcome here,' we mean it. And that is because Jesus didn't' reject anyone, and neither do we.

God's Spirit has blessed this church with the kind of love open to all people! In that, it is the kind of love that calls upon us to be 'a people' of prayer! Praying that by God's Holy Spirit, we can continue to be the church of Jesus Christ, who shares the Good News about the love that God has for each of us in our church, and *for all people*.

Friends, people all around us are hurting and need the all-embracing love we have here at Union as the Spirit came to remind us all of God's ever-present love that is with all of creation. God's love does not discriminate based on race, gender, loving preferences, religion, zip code, socioeconomic status, or immigration status. And neither do we.

And we know this because of John 3:16, NIV, which says that God so loved the world it did not say, this kind or that kind the Bible says, that God loved the world that He gave His only begotten Son. So, when people use the Bible to justify their racism, sexism, homophobia, and any other manufactured division, quote that scripture and offer the knowledge of God's love for us all.

We hear this kind of love echoed by today's psalmist, who sings of God's Spirit breathing life upon all creatures and even renewing the face of the ground.

And so, when our hearts are unmoving, and our souls complain, may God's Spirit renew us. When our ears are clogged, and our bones are exhausted, may God's Spirit renew us. And when our minds say "no" and we have lost our willpower to try, may God's Spirit renew us. And may we continue to embrace the loving Spirit of God in our own lives so that we can remain united and uniting in Christ, towards ourselves, one another, and amongst all creation. **AMEN**.

PRAYER

Holy God, the earth is full of your love. May we, your children, born of the Spirit, bear witness to your Son Jesus Christ, crucified and risen, that all the world may believe and have eternal life through the One who saves, now and forever. Amen.

LETTER NINE

This is Good

Are we willing to accept God's invitation to love all creation?

<u>June 7, 2020</u>
<u>Trinity Sunday (First Sunday after Pentecost)</u>

THIS IS GOOD
On this blessed Trinity Sunday, we are here celebrating the mysterious encounter of God's presence in our lives! As Jesus shares, when we encounter the triune God, known as the Father, Son, and Holy Spirit, we become new people, and THIS IS GOOD!

And in hearing this, we might ask, **"Are we willing to accept God's invitation, to love all creation?"**

Jesus reminds us of the importance of our baptism <u>first, to strengthen our relationship with God so that we might secondly go out and spread God's love towards others.</u>

An old tale helps explain God's trinity from today's lesson. The story tells of a man enjoying the preacher's difficulty explaining it! [22]

And I can relate to this story because it is not easy to explain all of who God is, in that, God is infinite beyond the grasp of our limited minds. And we may be able to study nature objectively and form theories about how the universe came into existence. Still, it is beyond the scope of human reason when it comes to understanding God!

But that does not mean that we cannot know God! As Jesus is saying in his conversation with the disciples, if we genuinely want to know God and experience his kingdom, it can happen as we enter into a relationship with God. The actual knowledge of God cannot be obtained from an objective distance, as if we were studying science, but through an intimate understanding, which comes to us as God embraces us and adopts us into a family of faith.

Thus, if we want to know God, we can be open to the power of God's Spirit, which we receive through our baptism. Whether we were baptized as an infant or baptized as an adult, it is God's Spirit that calls us into a relationship with God and with the church here on earth.

There is little doubt that Jesus' words refer to baptism as the entry point of our relationship with God. As Jesus says, "Very truly I tell you, no one can enter the kingdom of God [or even come to know God] without being born of water and the Spirit." [23] Thus, it is through our baptism that we receive the new birth, become a member of Christ's church, and are empowered by God's Spirit to grow in our understanding of God.

And with these things in mind, let us return to our question, **"Are we willing to accept God's invitation, to love all creation?"**

In our response, we can open our hearts for God to dwell within our lives and humbly accept God's call to care and to be caretakers of one another and the Earth is the message Jesus conveys to the disciples.

As God's Spirit is like the wind, and that is why we hear Jesus invites the disciples to be open to this uncontrollable but trustworthy Presence of God. As the wind is all around us but unseen, so too is God all around us but unseen.

And as part of God's creation, we are asked to live amongst creation with compassion and grace because we are God's image of love. Yes, each one of us is in God's image. Yes, that means that God did not make any mistakes when creating us. Yes, that means when God created us, God said THIS IS VERY GOOD!! [24]

So, the next time we look at ourselves in the mirror. Let us know that God loves us despite the wrongs we have done in our past, but we are to seek forgiveness. Let us know that God loves us despite our fallen in our faith walk, but we are to reach out for a helping hand. And let us know that God loves us despite the times when we have had to bear witness time and time again that black lives do not matter so that we can remain encouraged, in the struggle for justice and peace, for equal treatment of humanity, everywhere.

And to make sure that we all know of God's love for us all, Jesus tells the disciples to go out and baptize others as Jesus wants it to be clear that God's love is for the whole world, not just for a select few.

Jesus knows their fears and insecurities because they are huddled together in the upper room, where they feel safe. But, Jesus tells them to let go of the known and allow the Spirit-wind of God to envelop them. In that, it is the wind that we cannot see, and it is the wind that we cannot touch, and yet, it is the wind that we can feel, and it is the wind that we can hear.

This encounter of being baptized that Jesus speaks of is a daily process of being re-created, daily, in God's image. Because, with each passing day, we have a new opportunity to live in the created image of love's God. And yet, with each day, we face a new world of new possibilities. In that, being born anew means that we recommit ourselves to our faith in God so that no matter what happens, or regardless of what we have done with God's help, we can start again as Jesus invites us all, to renew our faith, every day.

Being born anew speaks to those times when we feel lost or alone or in those times when we think that we have nothing to show for all our best efforts. Being born anew can also speak to when we show our love for God but feel that God is somehow distant from us or when we feel like our spiritual life is not what we want it to be. As these are the times when we can ask for God to come into our hearts, and if today is one of those times, we can ask for God to come into our hearts right now.

Because, if we are willing to open our hearts and allow God's Spirit to work in us, and through us, to give us anew birth and a new life, we will be made fresh again in the wonder of God's love as we are all created, in God's image. And all in search of a revolution from an unjust system, THIS IS GOOD!!

Because while we must vote, no matter how hard we try, we cannot legislate hearts. That is why we need to KEEP PRAYING for the Spirit of God to lead the way!!!

And that is why the wind is like the Holy Spirit. In our lives, we cannot see it. We do not know where it goes, and we cannot even explain how it works, but it is here for us to experience God working in each of our lives.

Our lives and faith should not stagnate when we remain in a close relationship with God. Therefore, our belief is changing and evolving each day.

There is a story about living in a close relationship with God. And to follow God's guidance of the Spirit, a giant oak tree that was uprooted by the wind and thrown across a stream. And when it fell among some Reeds, it asked, "I wonder how you, who are so light and weak, are not entirely crushed by these strong winds."

And the Reeds replied, "You fight and contend with the wind and consequently break; while we on the contrary bend before the least breath of air, and therefore remain unbroken, and escape." [25]

Friends, we, too, have a choice. We can give in to the power of the Spirit in our lives and bend with the "wind" as it leads us, or we can resist and break and become our guide. Jesus teaches us that the Spirit will lead us in truth if we let it. As Jesus suggests that we resist trying to figure out where the Spirit will lead or how it will lead, but Jesus, instead, calls upon us to simply open our hearts and allow God's Spirit to lead the way. And THIS... IS GOOD.

It is good because God's love is so good. God's love will carry us through every moment and guide us every day. As God's goodness reminds me of the old hymn, Lift Every Voice and Sing, by James Weldon Johnson, which says, 'God of our weary years, God of our silent tears, thou who has brought us thus far, on the way thou who has by thy might, led us into the light, keep us, forever, in the path, we pray.' May it be so. **Amen.**

PRAYER

Healing God help us accept your call to love and support one another. Teach us how to sacrifice our comfort to serve the needs of our hurting world better. Pour out your compassionate Spirit upon all people granting us vision, strength, and joy for this work so that we live out your justice and sing a new song of your great peace. **Amen.**

LETTER TEN

Sacrifice

What sacrificial work are we being called to carry out?

<u>Sunday, June 14, 2020</u>
<u>Second Sunday after Pentecost</u>

Sacrifice
On this second Sunday, after Pentecost, we witness people called by God to perform extraordinary acts which require a willingness to sacrifice one's comfort by serving God and others.

And so, we ask, **"What sacrificial work are we being called to carry out today?"**

The scriptures call upon us <u>to first have compassion by sacrificing our comforts to, secondly, better serve the needs of others.</u>

In that, trusting in God to perform extraordinary acts is at the heart of our message for today as we see this, in the story of Sarah and Abraham, when they were called by God, to trust that Sarah will give birth even, in her older age. Sarah and Abraham had to sacrifice control of their expectations and trust in God. And God's promise to them to birth a child is fulfilled when Isaac is born.

Trusting in God reminds us that we are not working alone. Trusting in God reminds us of the importance of doing what God calls us to do and trusting that God will bless it. In other words, when we get tired, we can rest from time to time, trusting that God will bless the work we are doing on God's behalf.

There is a story about a businessman who tells an angler to build a big fishing business to relax one day. But, the fisherman replied, "What do you think I am doing now!" [26]

This story about our trusting in God, even during our worries and our best efforts, reminds us to rest and be assured that God's vision will reign. Therefore, our sacrifice in living out the call that God has for us is to trust that we are not alone in the work that God has for us to do.

Trusting in God is the message that Jesus gave the disciples when He sent them out to preach the Good News, telling them that the Kingdom of God is near. [27] Because Jesus knew that having the disciples go and do this work would result in conflict.

Jesus knew that they would be afraid when the disciples ran into inevitable opposition. And He knew that they would worry.

Jesus called the disciples to preach the Gospel of God's equal love for everyone with boldness and told them to rely on God for their protection.

So, then, let's go back to our question, **"What sacrificial work are we being called to carry out today?"**

Jesus also calls upon us to serve God by spreading the Good News message and trusting that God will lead the way forward.

And this is exampled when Jesus saw the crowd had compassion for them and sent out the disciples to carry on His ministry to the shepherd-less— saying that the groups were like sheep without a shepherd. And by doing so, Jesus affirms that we all need love, like that of a compassionate shepherd.

As God is calling us individually, and as the church, to be the shepherds who care for others, by bringing the Good News that suffering ultimately leads to hope, rather than despair. This hope was exampled during our church's online Panel on Racism last week; we heard a diversity of thoughts on the topic, yet the common undertone was clear: there needs to be a message of God's love for everyone, shared in this world today.

We seek to live out the call that God has upon this church to sacrifice our comfort in a hurting world by doing the hard work of creating an opportunity for affordable senior housing on our church campus. We seek to live out God's call upon this church to sacrifice our comfort in a hurting world by doing the complex word of maintaining our mercy ministries of feeding the hungry and housing families in need of shelter.

We seek to live out the call that God has by engaging with one another on matters of injustice; having holy conversations by doing justice through education and action and visiting historical landmarks that remind us of the importance of having courage in the struggle, for justice and peace.

But, most of all, we seek to live out the call that God has upon our lives by continuously praying that equal justice for all will one day come and bring about Godly peace.

God cares for us all, which is the Good News message in the sermon that Jesus gave to the disciples. And because of this, we can pray for God to relieve us of our worries and help us see more clearly, the path that we are to take along our life's journey.

There is a quote from Dr. Charles Mayo of the famous Mayo Clinic about worrying, which says, "There is a growing mountain of evidence that worry is the chief contributor to depression, nervous breakdowns, high blood pressure, heart attacks, and early death." Then, he goes on to say, "I've never known a man die from hard work, but I have known a lot who have died from worry." [28]

And therefore, we hear the voice of the psalmist who shares with us today that God hears our cry. God knows us to the point of counting the number of hairs on our head; that is the kind of detailed interest that God has for every one of us!!

In that, we can bring our problems to God because God hears us, God knows us, and God loves us. The challenge for us is, "Who is in control of my life?" Is it God, or do I have to rely on my efforts?

But, if the Lord is No. 1 in our lives, then we are to resist our natural tendency to be afraid. And we can do this by taking a step back from the situation and bringing it to God in prayer.

Prayer is our way of saying, 'Healing God, I know you love me, and I know you want to guide me in every situation. But, I am struggling and need help.' As Jesus is our example, He did not worry. Instead, he regularly took a moment away from others to pray. We are all invited to sacrifice some of our time to do the same.

And so, let us continue to embrace the loving Spirit of God in our lives. Let us remain alive as one body, united and uniting in Christ, as we aim to continue to do the work of carrying God's love and care into the world, sacrificing our comforts, yet, trusting in God to sustain and guide us, along the way! May it be so. **Amen.**

PRAYER

Jesus, you call us to live our faith, traveling beside you. In a world filled with tension, you bring peace to the world. May we be reminded of your constant love for us and feel your presence in our lives as a reminder that we are loved as cherished children of God. **Amen.**

LETTER ELEVEN

Daring Disciples

In what ways should we dare to put God first in our daily lives?

Sunday, June 21, 2020
Third Sunday after Pentecost

Daring Disciples
On this Father's Day Sunday, we hear Jesus encouraging His disciples to remain faithful as daring disciples by telling them that no matter what the circumstances may be, put God first because God hears, and God cares, about them.

And as we think about Jesus' message to His disciples, we ask, **"In what ways should we dare, put God first, in our lives today?"**

The scriptures suggest that we first believe that God has a purpose and a plan for our lives so that we can secondly remember to put God first in all that we do.

On this Father's Day, we hear the story of Abraham, who faces a difficult decision concerning his two sons. However, it is essential to note that this story is about God's promise to Abraham. In that, he would become the father of many nations. [29] But, because of his wife, Sarah's advanced age... they did not believe that God's promise was possible, without having someone else to birth, a son, with Abraham.

And so, they decided to have their Egyptian house servant, Hagar, serve as a surrogate of sorts in birthing a son, whom they named Ishmael. But, after they decided to have a surrogate, Sarah becomes pregnant, and births a son, whom they call, Isaac. And therefore, we hear in today's passage that Sarah tells Abraham to send Hagar and Ishmael away because Sarah did not want Ishmael to share in the inheritance of Isaac.

But, Abraham was the father of both sons. He was filled with stress because he did not know what to do. After hearing from God, Abraham is comforted during his distress. He had the assurance from God that both of his sons would have nations of their own. For this reason, many believe that Abraham is the Father of Judaism through Isaac and that Abraham is the Father of Islam through Ishmael, along with being the Father of Christianity through Jesus as a descendant of David's lineage. That is why he is known by many as 'Father Abraham.' [30] In that, we are all known as being part of the Abrahamic religions. And yes, we're all connected, as God's call was for Abraham to be a daring disciple for the greater purpose.

To further example this message of believing in God's purpose and plan for our lives, we also see that Hagar also is filled with distress and cried out to God to save her son, who is dying. And once again, God speaks [31] and tells Hagar to keep going and keep trusting in the purpose for her and her son, Ishmael. And like Abraham, Hagar becomes a daring disciple and obeys.

Now, let us return to our question, **"In what ways should we dare put God first in our lives today?"**

In that, we can be daring enough to put God first, in every possible way!!! Being brave enough to put God first is the message in the story of Abraham, Sarah, and Hagar.

And we know that even as people of faith, there are times when we need to cry out to God for help amid our distress. We cry out, like Abraham, Hagar, and even like our psalmist today, who says, 'Incline your ear O Lord, and answer me… for I am poor and needy.' [32] As the psalmist goes on to say, because of you, O God, you have helped me and have comforted me.' [33]

How many of us have cried out to the Lord and have been comforted? We are comforted because we believe that we are not in this situation alone. We are comforted because a voice speaks to us and tells us to be the daring disciples of loving our neighbor as we love ourselves even when it brings us distress. After all, God has a purpose and a plan for all our lives and putting God first as daring disciples is just what Jesus teaches to the disciples today. Jesus is teaching them to become bold disciples of Godly love and to share it with the world. Jesus is encouraging them to go public with the message of putting God first in our lives. Jesus is telling them not to be silenced by the threats of bullies and the attention that they will bring to them. Jesus is reminding them of the purpose promised to them just as it was with Abraham, Sarah, and Hagar by telling them about the promise of something more wonderful than they can see or imagine.

Jesus Christ came so that we all might know that we are all one human race, loved equally by God. And this is the message that Christians who follow Jesus are to spread.

It is a message of love and not one of hate. It is a message of inclusion and not one of exclusion. That is why Jesus says, 'If your first concern is after yourself then, you'll never find yourself. But if you forget about yourself and look to me, you'll find both yourself and me.' [34] In other words, put God first, period.

But, sometimes, it is hard to be daring, especially during the storm, as there was a time when Jesus and the disciples were in the boat together during a terrible storm. And during this awful storm, Jesus was asleep. So, when the disciples saw that Jesus was sleeping, they wondered how He could sleep through the storm, and they asked how he could sleep when they were in danger. Their expectation was for him to be attentive to their needs and not be off somewhere asleep while living in fear.

But, we can feel like those disciples when it seems that during our crisis, God is off somewhere taking a nap. But, in the story, when the disciples awaken Jesus. He rebukes the storm and blames his disciples by asking them two questions. "Why are you so afraid?" and "Why do you still have no faith?"

But, of course, we can imagine the disciples saying we are fearful because of the raging storm, we are afraid because of the incredibly intense rocking of the boat, and the water swamping the boat, so much so that it was starting to sink. As it would seem, they have a right to be anxious.

But Jesus was hoping that, what they had seen Him do in the past, would provide a stronger faith in God for the future, but that was not the case. So, first, Jesus had to calm the storm, and then, he had to calm his disciples and remind them of the importance of trusting in God.

In that, Jesus saw that even these daring disciples, who left everything to follow Him, were afraid because they could only see the storm. Their eyes were on that storm. It was difficult for them to have peace when they focused on the storm, even though they were all in the boat together with Jesus.

The problem for the disciples, like us today, is not simply the storms of life but where we place our attention. Maybe that is why God is rocking the boat in the storms of our lives. Our boat is being rocked right now by the COVID-19 virus and the systemic racism as both pandemics are moving us by the Spirit-wind and forcing us to change course towards a new way forward. God is the captain of the Sea, who hears every disparaging cry and asks us to place our attention on the one thing that matters most, and that is, putting God first.

Focusing on God above all else will ultimately calm every storm, even those storms that intensely test our faith because God loves us all and has placed us in this boat together as the beloved children of God. So, when we face the storms of life, we need not be afraid or full of despair and give up on hope because God is with us and has the power to guide our lives into the ways of justice, love, and peace.

Some of us are experiencing emotional storms raging in our lives. Others of us know friends or loved ones who may feel alone, like Hagar, due to health concerns, relationship troubles, or financial difficulties. Yet, we are to remember that Jesus is with us. He calls us when we turn our eyes on the storm. He asks us to hear His words, "Peace! Be still. I am with you even to the ends of the earth." [35] He asks us to not only hear these words but to believe them as well.

But, this peace is not passive. It is active. It is a deep peace that reminds us that God's purpose will supersede life's messes. It is a deep peace that reminds us that the storm we are all facing together in the boat right now might change us for the better, and therefore, we are not to be afraid. An active peace reminds us to put God first, even if that means we are at odds with our loved ones who do not understand how to love our neighbor as we love ourselves. As ACTIVE PEACE reminds us, the way to heaven is through our acts of LOVE, which is in the life and teaching of Jesus Christ.

And so, let us know that God is with us today, and always loving us and caring for us even in those times when it seems like God has fallen asleep and has forgotten about us. But, even in those moments, let our prayers continue so that we hear God speaking purpose into our lives, as we seek to live boldly, joyfully, and faithfully as daring disciples in the steadfast love of God. May it be so. **AMEN.**

PRAYER

Welcoming God, you graciously love us as we are, and you model how we should be with each other. May you be patient with us and help us as we seek to understand what your genuine welcome and your hospitality mean for how we should be in our communities. We pray this in Jesus' name. **Amen.**

LETTER TWELVE

Holy Welcome

How can we show a holy welcome towards all people?

<u>Sunday, June 28, 2020</u>
<u>Fourth Sunday after Pentecost</u>

Holy Welcome
Today, we hear Jesus speaking with the disciples about the importance of offering a holy welcome to all people. As Jesus shares with the disciples, acts of kindness help people feel genuinely welcome by believers of God.

And as we think about Jesus' message to His disciples, we might ask, **"How can we show a holy welcome towards all people?"**

The scripture suggests people feel welcome when people of faith <u>show simple acts of kindness in the ways that God has demonstrated loving-kindness towards us.</u>

Many of us know what it is like to be the new kid. Or to go off school into a new environment. If anyone has ever felt the desire to feel welcomed, that is what Jesus is referring to in today's message, as we all need to feel welcomed when we come with our hearts open, to be received by others who represent what is good.

As I am sure that many of us have heard the phrase, kindness can take you a long way, but did you know that it could take you to heaven?

Well, that is what Jesus is telling His disciples. Jesus is calling upon the disciples to share the peace of God with someone else so that another might experience God's joy as Jesus is calling the disciples to extend the kind acts of love that they do for one another out into the world.

And as believers today, we are also being called to show God's love through our acts of kindness towards others. But, to do so, we are to remain humble.

Humility also occurs in a story about a hotel clerk in Philadelphia who met a couple in desperate need of a room. And when the clerk gave up his room, the couple was so grateful that they offered to build a luxurious hotel he would be able to manage. After the clerk agreed, his guest introduced himself as John Jacob Astor, and shortly after that, he built the Waldorf-Astoria Hotel. [36]

The point of this story is not that simple acts can show the love of God. In that, we see how one clerk chose to offer a simple act of kindness to strangers by sharing his room with this tired couple and touching them in ways he could not have foreseen. His simple act of kindness touched the fabric of this couple and significantly impacted how they looked at this young man.

Let us return to our question, **"How can we show a holy welcome towards all people?"**

As it seems, when we offer the best of what we have, we offer a Holy Welcome to God. And that is why Jesus says, whoever welcomes you, welcomes me. [37] As we are to find the strength and courage, to love others in the ways Jesus came, to show love for us.

But sometimes, it might be hard to reflect on the kind of love that God has for us. Sometimes we might find it challenging to greet someone with a smile, let alone serve them. And sometimes, when we do, it might even seem inadequate at times, especially when compared to the sacrifices Jesus

Christ made for us. But, when Jesus teaches us that giving a cup of water to someone is good, we can know that we are to serve people, regardless of who they are, and we offer them our Holy Welcome.

But, to offer a Holy Welcome, we need to welcome God into our hearts. Today's reading between God and Abraham was about God's close and loving relationship. In that, we are to put God first, above all things trusting in God's purpose and grace.

Today's psalmist also shares this message of welcoming God into our hearts, who sings of the pain in our souls that can shake our faith. This song reminds us that God is big enough to hear every thought embedded in our hearts, and because of this, we can rejoice in the steadfast love of God, which is always present.

Our welcome message is what we try to live out here at Union. The kind of holy welcome that receives all people into this faith family. We faithfully live into Jesus Christ's call for all believers: love God and love one another as we love ourselves.

This message of holy welcome is in the Louvre, located in Paris, where there is a famous painting by Murillo titled "The Miracle of San Diego." [38] As the painting shows, a door opens, and two noblemen and a priest enter a kitchen. And as they enter, they are amazed to find that all the kitchen maids are angels. One is handling a water pot, another a rack of meat, the third has a basket of vegetables, and the fourth is tending the fire.

The picture's message indicates that every act of service is valuable. But, not only is it beneficial, it is HOLY!!! As this picture reminds us, serving others is doing Godly work.

Here, at Union, we trust that God will continuously lead us along the right paths. Like our fantastic children who joined at Vacation Bible School in song and in Word to worship God. And in doing so, they held great discussions about the theme "We Are the World" and what that meant to them as children. They all agreed that God was calling on them to find ways to make a difference right now!! And, all that I can say is, watch out, world!!!!

Like the children, our adults also gather, as the Body of Christ, and call upon God to lead the way as we prepare to vote on whether to move forward with our Affordable Senior Housing Project. In that, it is a blessing to have acreage available on our church campus that could potentially serve our senior neighbors, in need, of affordable housing.

The scriptures teach us to offer a Holy Welcome to all because we are all the beloved children of God regardless of who we are or our backgrounds. As Jesus says, when we welcome all people, we receive Him. [39]

So then, let us open our hearts wide to receive God's long arms of welcome, care, and love. And as our hearts draw closer to God, let us also offer the same kind of welcome, care, and love towards others. **May it be so. AMEN.**

PRAYER

Jesus, you invite us to live our faith with the freedom of traveling beside you. May we be reminded of your constant love for us. May we feel your presence in our lives as a reminder that we are known and loved as cherished children of God. **Amen.**

Chosen Journeys

How might we open our hearts to love others courageously?

<u>Sunday, July 5, 2020</u>
<u>Fifth Sunday after Pentecost</u>

Chosen Journeys
Today, we hear Jesus inviting the crowd surrounding Him and telling them about the importance of their chosen journeys. As Jesus speaks of freedom, we all must choose courageous love in how we accept and receive others.

And as we think about Jesus' message to the crowd, we might ask, **"How can we offer our hearts to demonstrate courageous love toward others?"**

The scripture suggests that we <u>first surrender ourselves to God so that we can secondly choose to renew our trust in God.</u>

We have spent years working to help affect change for many of us as we can look back to writings and footage of marches, protests, and campaigns that seek to reach the consciousness of a people. But, at some point in our lives, it seems as if the more we try to make this world a better place, the harder it seems to get until we learn to surrender ourselves to God.

The story about a lifeguard's rescue of an athlete struggling to get out of the lake shows he could not save him until the athlete relinquished control. [40]

This story of struggle and exhaustion before deliverance is not only a lesson for lifeguards, but it is a powerful revelation of what often occurs in our spiritual journey. Some of us may feel spiritually exhausted, worn out, or weary of trying to please God with our efforts. And when we think this way, Jesus gives us great news. As He says, in Matthew 11:28, KJV, 'Come to Me, all you who labor and are heavily laden, and I will give you rest.'

And in addition to being at rest spiritually, Jesus also shares that because of this peaceful rest; we can live freely by having a close relationship with God. Trusting that God is with us, and when we need to rest, God will carry us forward, each step of the way. The famous poem, Footprints, [41] illustrates this beautifully when it says…

One night I had a dream - I dreamed I was walking along the beach with the Lord, and across the sky flashed scenes from my life.

For each scene, I noticed two sets of footprints. One belonged to me and the other to the Lord. When the last stage of my life flashed before me, I looked back at the footprints in the sand. I noticed that there was only one set of prints many times along my life path.

I also noticed that it happened at the lowest and saddest times in my life. This scene bothered me, and I questioned the Lord about it. 'Lord, you said that once I decided to follow you, you would walk with me all the way, but I have noticed that during the most troublesome times in my life, there is only one set of footprints. I don't understand why in times when I needed you most, you should leave me.'

Then, the Lord replied, 'My precious, precious child, I love you, and I would never, never leave you during your times of trial and suffering. When you saw only one set of footprints, it was then that I carried you.'

Now, let us go back to our question, **"How can we offer our hearts to demonstrate courageous love toward others?"**

We can follow what Jesus Christ calls upon us all to do: love, like Him. In that, trusting in the courageous love modeled by Jesus will help us make the stranger, our friend who could transcend our inner fears and societal boundaries, into an ever-expanding sense of connection and love.

When it seems our burdens are heavy to bear, this text assures us that we are not alone with these burdens.

As Jesus says in our language, come to me all who are struggling with life in any way, all who have burdens that cannot be carried alone, and I will help you with your struggles. In that, trusting in God is the chosen journey that God has for us all!

As Jesus wants us to come and place our burdens on Him so that we will be free to live life anew and enjoy life by sharing Jesus' life with others and because of this, others might also experience the great good news of Christ's love, in their life's journey.

Today's scriptures emphasize our need to offer kindness and hospitality towards one another, even the stranger. This kindness is exampled in the Genesis reading. We see that Rebekah gives water to a stranger who was the servant of Abraham, and now, to his son, Isaac. We learn that Rebekah's act of kindness is the beginning of a great love story between Rebekah and Isaac.

The need for showing kindness towards one another is also exampled in the Psalm when we hear the retelling of Rebekah's story, which says, 'I will cause your name to be celebrated in all the nations.' [42] Hospitality, even in the smallest ways, can transform our community and even our own lives in beautiful and unforeseeable ways.

As people who have shared our lives with the Lord, we also can be willing to listen to the life stories of one another. We can share in our peacefulness, walk beside one another in our respective journeys to share something of ourselves, and share that Christ will help make our burdens lighter.

We are called together as the body of Christ, not as an isolated island, but as a living working body that shares the hurts, the heartaches, and the problems we encounter.

An illustration of this is in the old story, which tells how a man came upon a small child carrying an even smaller child on his back, paralyzed. And the man says, 'That's a heavy burden for you to carry.' The child responds, saying, 'That's no burden. He's my little brother.'

Jesus shows us how to carry our heavy loads to help others with their load. As our choice to love, like Jesus guides us, when He says,

'Come to me, all who labor and are heavily laden, and I will give you rest. Take my yoke upon you and learn from me, for I am gentle and lowly in heart, and you will find rest for your shoulder. For my yoke is easy, and my burden is light.' [43] Our choice to trust God in this way is to live in true faith.

We are to do our best but not allow it to become our burden. We can choose to take our hopes, dreams, worries, fears, weariness, pain, exhaustion, sadness, anxieties, stress, every form of injustice, our quest for peace, and everything we desire to God in prayer and leave it, right, there.

We can choose to leave it there, trusting that God will enter our hearts, provide for our every need, and give us spiritual rest.

May we choose to allow God's love to carry and renew us as we seek to love all people, even the stranger, courageously. Amen.

PRAYER

God of mercy, you are full of tenderness and compassion, slow to anger, rich in mercy, and always ready to forgive. Grant us grace to be like you and to live together in love. **Amen.**

LETTER FOURTEEN

Wheat and Weeds Together

How does God want us all to live together?

Sunday, July 19, 2020
Seventh Sunday after Pentecost

Wheat and Weeds Together

Today, we hear Jesus speaking among the crowd telling another story about a farmer who planted good seeds in his field, but later evil came along and planted weeds alongside the wheat. Jesus explains the importance of God's love for us all by encouraging them to live alongside one another, like **wheat and weeds together,** in the field.

As we think about this story, our question becomes, **"How does God want all of us to live together?"**

In looking at the scripture, it suggests that we can first accept God's challenge into a new way of being, to secondly, open space for God's justice, peace, and love, to be received by the world.

As this message about the wheat and the weeds is a clear reminder, God is aware of the injustices, tension, and evil that exist, alongside all that is good.

There was plenty of evil in Jesus' time. If Jesus had asked any of his disciples what some of those evils were, they could have pointed out a dozen social problems.

But, the disciples' way of dealing with those problems was different from God's way. They thought they would overcome the Romans by pulling the weeds, which symbolized the enemy. Many felt that they could fight their way into the kind of kingdom that would please God as they did with kings of the Old Testament such as King Solomon and King David.

But, Jesus spread the Good News of God by preaching and teaching that God is calling everyone into the eternal Kingdom of Love.

The disciples saw themselves as being good, like the wheat. But, Jesus teaches them that there are weeds in the field. In that, Jesus points out that this parable speaks about God loving everyone, even those who have allowed evil, into their hearts.

Many feel that evil does not exist, and in fact, some are ministers. And it is usually the elders of the church who watch and wait for the new minister to understand firsthand that they may experience unpleasant experiences along the journey. But, of course, that was not about any devils existing in this church.

But, in all seriousness, no one is perfect, and Jesus is making this message clear even to the believers. Indicating that we all tend to be like weeds, but when we embrace God's presence in our lives, we can become like wheat, for God.

And so, when encountering the tension between good and evil in our lives, we can adopt the strategy of Paul, who said in Romans 12:21, "Do not be overcome by evil but overcome evil, with good."

We see the goodness of God, for example, today, in Jesus' parable. Rather than risk damaging the wheat, by getting rid of the weeds, the farmer who is, God decides, that the wheat and weeds will remain together.

Now, let us go back to our question, **"How does God want all of us to live together?"**

We can simply seek the courage to choose good over evil by opening our hearts and minds to receive a new relationship with God and with one another even, our enemies.

The challenge of choosing good over evil is in a story from Philip Yancey's book, "Soul Survivor," about a lesser-known man named Rev. John Perkins, a minister in the South, who "lived through the worst nightmares of the civil rights movement." [44]

Perkins started a church, then a Bible Institute launched a radio program, established a health clinic, a vocational training center, a recreational center for youth, an after-school tutoring program, and a housing program. But, when he started a voter registration campaign and led an economic boycott to protest police brutality in downtown Mendenhall, Mississippi, he crossed the line.

And they let him know he crossed the line when the Reverend was attacked by more than a dozen white policemen and beaten so severely that doctors had to remove 2/3 of his stomach, and as a result, it took him 18 months to recover.

And in response to this attack, Perkins shared, 'That, time, was without a doubt, [his] most profound crisis of faith. It was time for [him] to decide if [he] did believe, what [he] had so often professed that only, in the love of Christ, not, in the power of violence is there any hope for [him], or the world.

[As he] began to see how hate could destroy [him]. And in the end, [he] had to agree with Dr. King [who preached] that God wanted us to return good for evil. [And that is why], Jesus said, "Love, your enemy." [45] And he was determined to do it as Jesus' concept of love overpowers hate.

[Perkins went on to say,] I may not see it in my lifetime. But, I know, it is true. Because on that bed, full of bruises and stitches, God made it true to me. I got a transfusion of hope. I could not give up." (p 35)

Several years later, Perkins found himself, back in Mississippi, as God would have it. There, he spearheaded a movement for racial reconciliation and often appeared with "Thomas Tarrants, a Ku Klux Klan operative, who served time for murder got converted in prison, and now pastors a multiracial church, in Washington, D.C." (35).

For Perkins, it was clear that violent acts could not shake the sin, of racism, out of neighbors. But, instead, loving them, even to the point of death, could affect the kind of change needed; not a violent change, but a change towards love, a change of heart.

As if God were to rip all the evil out of the world, God would pull all of us out, right along, with it. So, rather than be overcome by evil, we need to recognize it for what it is and use it well. In other words, we can choose to use a terrible temptation, evil action, or a difficult person as an opportunity to rise above it, rather than respond in kind and give into it.

In that, Jesus reminds us not to worry when we experience trouble in this world, as He says, "Take courage [because], I, have overcome, the world." [46]

There are times when we can feel defeated and discouraged because the forces of evil that seem to grow on their own can overwhelm us.

In our waking, sleeping, loving, being loved in our working and our playing and everything that we do, we can throw our whole selves, upon the Love of God and, by our doing so we can continue, to overcome evil, with good!

We can be like Rev. Perkins and pray for the courage to seek justice and peace, in our lives, in our church, and throughout the world. We are a congregation that aims to be patient and loving towards all people. We are a church that believes God is good, all the time, even in those times, of hardship or uncertainty, because we think that God is good. We are like today's psalmist, who seeks life, led by God to guide the way.

And so, in our good times and in our bad times, let us embrace God's presence to help us grow spiritually. And as we grow spiritually, let us allow God to guide us into new possibilities of justice, peace, and love. And by our faith, let us trust that we are to coexist, like wheat and weeds together, trusting that we are all capable of yielding a great harvest because we are in God's love. Amen, and **AMEN.**

PRAYER

Spirit-God, we give you thanks for your Word planted in our hearts and for the yeast of love that you have mixed into our lives. Help us, we pray, to value all that you have given us and to follow the way of Christ in our lives so that we can do your will and share the Good News message of love spoken through your Son, Jesus Christ, our Lord.
Amen.

LETTER FIFTEEN

Weaving the Future

How can God's love weave into the hearts of believers today?

<u>Sunday, July 26, 2020</u>
<u>Eighth Sunday after Pentecost</u>

Weaving the Future

On this Sunday, Jesus shares short stories that refer to the generations of believers that are to come. As Jesus begins **weaving the future** into His message of faith, he uses four different comparisons about God's kingdom.

And as we think about these four examples that Jesus shares, we might ask, **"How can God's love weave into the hearts of believers today?"**

In looking at the scripture, it suggests that we <u>first value the love that God has freely given to us so that we can live according to the purpose God's love has for our lives.</u>

To get this message of God's love across to his listeners, Jesus talks about the kingdom of God. He uses mustard seed, describes yeast in flour, compares a Hidden Treasure, and examines a fishing net as Jesus teaches the believers to weave into their future faithfulness and love by trusting that God will help change and transform their lives.

For example, an old story about being transformed is told by a university dean. He felt like an angel appeared to him at a faculty meeting and told him that in return for his unselfish service, he would choose his choice of wealth, wisdom, or beauty. And without hesitating, the dean selects wisdom.

Then, the dean felt he heard the angel say, "It is done!" Then, the image disappeared into a cloud of smoke. And as anyone could imagine, all the other faculty members stared at the dean with amazement.

So, finally, one of them said to the dean, "Now, that you have infinite wisdom, say something." And the dean looked at them and said, "I should have taken the money." [47]

But in our lesson for today, Jesus is talking about a different kind of transformation. He invites the crowd of believers to transform their faith by choosing to look for the love that God freely offers to us all.

For example, there is a story about two people who experienced the same worship service but responded differently. The worship experience blesses one, and the other is unappreciative and cannot wait to leave.

As God's love is present and freely given on any given Sunday morning, it is how we choose to respond to God's love that determines how our hearts are changed so that we are ready for the future that God has for us all.

As Paul puts it, like this in Ephesians 2:8-10, NIV, 'For it is by grace, you have been saved, through faith and this is not from yourselves, it is the gift of God and not by works so that, no one can boast. For we, are God's workmanship, created in Christ, Jesus, to do good works which God prepared in advance, for us to do.'

The story of the two church visitors, as well as the stories that Jesus tells, seeks to open our hearts and our souls into the vastness of God's love. The smallest seed, faithfulness or the tiniest yeast, of believing in God's goodness can transform us and ultimately change our lives.

Now, let us go back to our question, **"How can God's love weave into the hearts of believers today?"**

Our response can be that we pray for God's love to weave inside each of us by giving us enough faith to trust that God will bring us through any and everything we encounter.

This weaving of love and faith is when we follow in the ways of God's love for ourselves and one another. And to make sure that his disciples understand this lesson, Jesus talks about faith by using a mustard seed because it was the tiniest possible seed. Yet, the fantastic thing about this tiny seed is that the plant can grow as high as 12 ft tall, which is more than twice most of our heights!

But, what is also remarkable about this story is that Jesus teaches this lesson to a tiny crowd of believers. Yet, today as much as a quarter to half of the world's population would call themselves Christian. This message of God's faithfulness and love is an excellent message for us all! It is a message of a future with God to remind us that by faith, we can get through every adversity, and because of this faith, in God, we can be at peace by trusting in God instead of being stressed out by worrying about our doubts, and fears.

Fanny Crosby is an excellent example of someone who had tremendous faith in God as a hymn writer. She gifted the world with more than 6,000 gospel songs. And although an illness blinded her at only six weeks old, she never showed signs of bitterness.

Some could not understand how Fannie was not upset for being blind. But, her faith shined through when she said, "Because, when I get to heaven, the first face, that shall ever, gladden, my sight will be that of my Savior!" [48]

Now, that is love because, even though Fanny could not see with her eyes, Fanny's faith showed her faithfulness in God. Fanny had opened her heart to truly see God so much so, that she looked forward to seeing the Lord, face to face in glory!!

And this is a kind of faithful love also seen in today's Genesis story about Jacob and Rachel. Jacob was known for his trickery, but, after finding love with Rachel, he was willing to do whatever, it took to be with her. And so, instead of being the one, who continued to trick others, he became the one tricked by Rachel's dad, which made him wait to be with Rachel for a total of 14 years.

Now, that is love, as Jacob was faithful in showing his love for Rachel. And what is so fascinating about this story is that in today's Psalm, we see God's purpose for Rachel and Jacob's love as we hear in the Psalm that the twelve tribes of Israel came from Jacob.

Jacob, transformed by love, understood what love means and how God had a greater purpose for his life.

And so, let us also trust that God will move us forward into the purpose-filled blessings that are equitable for all of humanity. Trusting that our future, of being woven together, as a human race, by Godly love is far beyond, what we know, or understand it, to be. So then, let us choose to trust in the teachings of Jesus Christ. Let us allow God's love to forever weave into our hearts so much so that we continuously become transformed by Godly wisdom, to understand better that what we do in our lives impacts not only ourselves but all of God's beloved creation. So, let the Spirit of God be our guide. May it be so. **AMEN.**

PRAYER

Loving God, when we are hungry, feeds us with bread and fish for the journey. When we struggle, sustain us with words of wisdom and stories of hope. And when we wrestle with unknown forces, touch us with companionship and love.
Amen.

LETTER SIXTEEN

Face to Face

In what ways do we experience being face to face with God?

Sunday, August 2, 2020
Ninth Sunday after Pentecost

Face to Face

On this Communion Sunday, we hear of Jesus feeding 5000 hungry people, and at that moment, the crowd realized that they were face to face with God's love.

And so, as we think about this famous Biblical story, our question becomes, **"In what ways do we experience being face to face with God today?"**

In looking at the scripture, it suggests that if we seek God's love, then we will be fed with hope for the journey.

If I were to take a poll of everyone listening to this sermon, it would be clear that most of us have heard about the loaves and fish story. And, since this story is such a popular story, I would like to approach it from a different perspective this morning by adding the version of John's gospel that mentions the 'little boy' in the story.

So, let us imagine we are that little boy with the loaves and fish.

As our day starts like any other day wandering around the hillside, we see this crowd gathering. And being little children, we follow the crowd as they gather around the seashore looking for Jesus. But since we are so small, we cannot see much, so we make our way to the front of the crowd to see better.

Then, we see Jesus get out of the boat, and He begins to talk to the crowd. So, like any curious child, we sit down on the grass to get comfortable and listen to Jesus.

Then, we hear Jesus teaching people about the kingdom of God. And we begin to think to ourselves that:

"Jesus is talking about God's love for all people, including me."

And after hearing these words, we get back up and start to walk around some more. Then, we notice some of Jesus' disciples in the crowd as they are helping people to come forward for healing. But, being children, we look up to the sky and notice that it is getting late, and we also realize that in all the excitement of the day, we forget to eat lunch.

So, we look for a spot to sit down again to eat our packed lunch, but we notice that no one else is eating.

Then, we overhear the disciples telling Jesus that they want to send the people away because there is not enough food to feed the crowd.

Then, we hear one of the disciples tell Jesus about our packed lunch filled with loaves and fish. And then, suddenly, we see the disciples coming towards us.

As we begin to wonder, "Why are they coming in this direction when there are only five small loaves of bread and two small fish?" And as a child, we continue with the question, "What could they possibly want with it because surely this small amount cannot feed the whole crowd."

But despite our questions, the disciples come to us and ask us to go with them to see Jesus face to face!

And so, we question whether to give Jesus our food because we are hungry, too. But, we trust that Jesus will do something more with the food, so we hand it over.

Then, the disciples take the loaves and fish from us and give them to Jesus. After receiving the food, we see Jesus ask the people to sit down, and then Jesus turns to heaven and prays.

And as we sit on the grass in front of Jesus, we see a marvelous thing happen. We see Jesus break the loaves and the fish and hands the food to the disciples to give to the people. And Jesus just keeps breaking bread and giving for what seems like forever.

Then, the disciples finally hand us some fish and bread, and there is enough for us to get seconds. And as we are eating, we watch the disciples gather 12 baskets and go about the crowd gathering the leftover food.

And as children, we are amazed to see the leftover food from our small lunch! As we see the disciples giving away these baskets of food to the very poorest people in the crowd so that they might have something to eat tomorrow.

And as we are watching all of this happen, we notice that the crowd is thinning out. Everyone is heading home, and we look toward the sky and see it is getting dark. So, we get up very full from our meal and begin to walk back home.

And as we walk home, we think, "This has indeed been an exciting day. As we heard Jesus tell about the kingdom of heaven, how He heals people who are hurting, and the two witnessed Jesus take our small lunch and make it into a meal to feed thousands of adults and children. And of course, we could hardly wait to tell the Good News to everyone we knew.

What a wonderful thing to imagine as children of God seeing Jesus face to face!! This story reminds us that God will help us with our needs if we turn over every need from our hands and put it all in God's hands.

Bringing us back to our question, **"In what ways do we experience being face to face with God today?"**

And our response can be a prayer for God to help us remember that there is an abundance of whatever it is that we need. In that, sometimes we worry about how enormous our need is, and God is telling us to trust and wait on the abundance.

Waiting on the abundance is what happened in the Genesis story with Jacob and God. We learn that Jacob is leaving his father-in-law's land and traveling back to his hometown of Canaan. Jacob thought he would come face to face with his estranged brother, Esau, and make peace, but Jacob ends up coming face to face with God on his journey home and attains true peace. As Jacob's name would become Israel and by his faith, Jacob's purpose would later become more significant than he had ever imagined.

So, where does all this leave us? It leaves us with a need to acknowledge our dependence on God. It leaves us with a need to realize our real need, which is to know God and accept the gift of Jesus Christ as the Bread of Life. It means that we rest genuinely in God, who can meet all our actual needs so that we can turn away from our fears and turn towards our faith in God.

And that is why Jesus said, "So, do not worry, saying, 'What shall we eat?' or 'What shall we drink?' or 'What shall we wear?' But seek his kingdom and righteousness first, and all these things will be given to you, as well. Therefore, do not worry about tomorrow, for tomorrow will worry about itself. Each day has enough trouble, of its own." (Matthew 6:25-34, NIV)

In that, we can be like the late Civil Rights champions John Lewis, C.T. Vivian, and others who made the most of each passing day by dedicating their lives towards peaceful measures, for the equal treatment, of all people. Today's psalmist lifts the importance of justice and peace by proclaiming that God supplies all our needs even when we get angry about all the injustices because we trust that God hears our cries as we can believe, just like the psalmist and those great Civil Rights leaders. God is big enough to take our anger and frustration and transform us with the hope that ultimately justice for all will come through God's everlasting mercy!!

We can trust that we will live into God's mercy for all people because we will be disciples of Jesus working together to accomplish God's purpose and plan. We can work together as part of this congregation to follow God's leading. We can be in partnership, with each other, and with God.

And as disciples of Jesus Christ, we are called to listen to God, trust in God, and shine God's light in the world by sharing, even if that share is small, by the world's standards. Because, when we partner with each other and with God, nothing is ever too big, and nothing is ever impossible. A great example of our stepping towards doing something positive is to honor those Civil Rights champions by making sure we all VOTE!!!

And so, let us remain hungry for God's Word, which calls upon us to love our neighbor as we love ourselves. Let us also be childlike in our faith, trusting that something more will come. And let us remember that whatever situation God leads us into, God will lead us through for the sake of equality, justice, and true peace until that glorious day when it is our turn to see Jesus Christ face to face. **May it be so. AMEN.**

PRAYER

Ever-present God, we encounter you amidst a broken world. You invite us into these spaces of brokenness – into these cracks, through which the light shines. Thank you for the gift of your presence, even in the difficulty of the unknown. **Amen.**

LETTER SEVENTEEN

When All Seems Lost

How can we hold on to hope in those times when all seems lost?

<u>Sunday, August 9, 2020</u>
<u>Tenth Sunday after Pentecost</u>

When All Seems Lost

This Sunday, we hear about stories of hope **when all seems lost** as we hear about Joseph, whose brothers mistreated him because of their jealousy. We also hear about when the disciples' doubts turn into belief and Jesus allows Peter to walk on water!

As we think about today's lessons, we might ask, **"How can we hold on to hope, especially in those times when all seems lost?"**

The scripture suggests that if <u>we believe that God's presence will help us overcome our doubts, we will tell others about God's faithfulness.</u>

And a perfect example of 'God being present in every situation is found in the story of Joseph that we hear today. And since Joseph was born when Jacob was older, he became Jacob's 'favorite' son. Because of this, Jacob shows a special love for Joseph by giving him what has become known as the beautifully ornamented 'coat of many colors.' [49] But Joseph's brothers did not handle this special relationship well at all. They hated Joseph for it, to the point where they could not speak a kind word to him.

And when Joseph revealed to his brothers the dreams that he had where they were bowing down to him, it only infuriated them even more. But, little did they realize that Joseph received a prophecy of what was to come. However, they thought he was "milking" his father's special love for himself for all it was worth!

And because of their jealousy and hatred of their brother, they first plotted to kill Joseph, then amended the plot to throw him into a pit, but later settled on selling him to be someone else's servant.

And what made it worse was that after selling their brother to traders, they now plot to hide their actions by making it look like a wild animal had attacked and killed Joseph. As we can imagine that when Jacob heard that his youngest son was dead, he felt that all seemed lost, but God was still with Jacob even when all the other sons stood there to watch their father's sadness because of their lie.

This story about Joseph reminds us of situations where we or someone we know just felt like throwing in the towel. We may have often said to ourselves, "No matter what I do, things still won't change." Or we may feel that we have gotten so far down that nothing can bring us up.

As we listen to the story, we hear how Joseph had been humiliated by his brothers and stood steadfast. The life of Joseph is an excellent example of the verse in Romans 8:28, KJV, which tells us that "we know that all things work together for good to them that love God, to them who are called according to his purpose."

The sale of Joseph by his brothers to become a servant to strangers was to cause him harm. But in the end, God is always with Joseph, and he becomes the ruler of Egypt. As a result, he forgives his brothers, reunites with them, and even saves their lives.

Now, back to our question, **"How can we hold on to hope, especially in those times when all seems lost?"**

Our response can be to trust in God's presence and purpose for our lives so that we can remain faithful like Joseph, who survives a problematic situation. God's presence is also in Jesus Christ, who saves the disciples on the rough waters just as God rescues Joseph in a strange land. And we can also trust that God will help us through every season of our lives.

Because like Joseph and the disciples we see in the stories today, we also experience situations meant to make us stop trusting God! Things intended to make us feel sorry for ourselves! Conditions intended to make us give up! Yes, there may be things designed to harm us, "But God" means them for our good! In that, God takes us through things to make us stronger!

And while sometimes we might not realize it but among the thorns, we generally will find a beautiful rose! Yes, some mean to harm us, "But God" will turn it around and create a life for us that is better than we know to ask for, and God will offer us more than we can ever imagine! And when we experience this kind of faithfulness from God, we can go off and tell others.

But before we tell others about God's presence in our lives, it is important to pray that God gives us the words to say to understand each other better.

A humorous story is told about a new preacher asking the farmer if he's a Christian, and the farmer replies he is a Jones. The Christians live down the street.

As it seems that instead of using phrases that some may not understand, the best thing to do is share our stories of how God helps us when all seems lost, as this is the way to help others learn about God's loving purpose for us all.

As telling of God's loving presence and purpose is just what the psalmist does in today's song as the words tell us that it was God who sent Joseph into Egypt, and it was God who gave Joseph the gift of interpreting dreams. As we see through the scripture, God's persistent presence and goodness continue despite the behavior of others or even despite ourselves when we prove to be less than perfect. Still, God uses it all to bring about our salvation!!

And so, may we believe that just as God provided for Joseph, and just as Jesus provided reassurance for the disciples, God's loving and saving grace also provides for us even when all seems lost. Trusting in God's presence and purpose so much so that we will be able to tell others about the goodness of God's faithfulness in our lives.

May it be so. **AMEN.**

PRAYER

Loving God be with us as we open ourselves to the word in scripture, the word in our hearts, and the word that binds us together. Help us be more open to our struggles as we learn about the struggles of others. May we be open to the challenges before us. **Amen.**

LETTER EIGHTEEN

Bold Moves

How can we make bold moves toward the plan God has for us?

Sunday, August 9, 2020
Eleventh Sunday after Pentecost

Bold Moves

Today, we hear more about the Old Testament story of Joseph and his brothers who mistreated him. Joseph's bold moves involved forgiving and reuniting with his brothers, revealing Joseph's faith in God's purpose and plan for his life.

As we think about this story, we might ask, **"How can we make bold moves toward the plan that God has for our lives?"**

In looking at the scripture, it suggests that when we suffer from the mistreatment of others, we are to 1) trust in God's plan for our lives and forgive them so that we can 2) begin to let go of the pain or resentment and begin to heal.

Forgiveness is a BOLD MOVE. As many of us know, forgiveness is not an easy task. But a necessary one for healing the soul.

For example, one Sunday, a Preacher's message was about forgiveness. For an impact, towards the end, the preacher asked, "How many of you have forgiven those who offended you?"

About half of the congregants raised their hands. And since only half raised their hands, the preacher felt there was more work to do. So, the preacher preached for another 20 minutes and asked again. This time, everyone raised their hands except one elderly lady seated in the back. And so, the preacher called out her name and said, "Mrs. Jones... Are you not willing to forgive your enemies?"

And she responded, "I am ninety-three years old and don't have a single enemy." The preacher responded by saying, "Wow, that is very unusual," and then asked if she wouldn't mind coming before the congregation to share her testimony of how the Lord helped her to forgive.

So, Mrs. Jones agreed, and strolled down the aisle, turned around to face the congregation, and said, "It's simple, I outlived them all."

But, when we seriously consider the act of forgiveness with the love of God in our hearts, we do not overlook the problem we face or evade the issue as we find that when power and authority come into play, it can cause separation. Jesus examples power and authority towards the Canaanite woman, [50] as He shares with the woman that his focus was not on her people. But, the woman did not back down from reminding Jesus about the evil that brought suffering upon her daughter. And at that moment, Jesus, himself, embraced the fullness of God's mercy for healing and unity. Jesus healed the woman's daughter and demonstrated God's love for all people.

The act of forgiveness reminds us all of God's love for us all. But, we are to approach forgiveness in truth and love. And we see this with Joseph and his brothers about their cruel act, when he says, in Genesis 45:4, NRSV, "I am your brother, Joseph, the one you sold, into Egypt." We notice that Joseph did not try to minimize or hide the truth. In other words, Joseph says to them, this cruel act is what separated us, but I am willing to forgive you and start all over, again.

Joseph's words to his brothers remind me of a message on a marquee that read, "God doesn't promise us a comfortable journey, just a safe landing." We hope that the last phrase of this sentence is true because we know from experience that the first part of the sentence is accurate and that none of us goes through this life without facing struggles and woundedness.

But, if we live an abundant life by moving beyond success to significance and being healed from life hurts, our wounds must heal and scar over, rather than fester and infect our whole being. A meaningful way for this to happen is to learn how to let go of our resentment.

And if there was ever a man who lived, who could be justified in his resentment, it was Joseph. He was born into a life of privilege, his father's favorite son. He was a great-grandson of Abraham. He was given the finer things in life, and he never had to work. Joseph was destined for a charmed life until his brothers sought to harm him. His brothers did not like Joseph's preferential treatment from their father, Jacob. Because of this, some of his brothers sought to kill Joseph but eventually settled for selling him into slavery.

Joseph could have sought revenge, but he did not. Instead, Joseph acknowledges God's hand in the actions of his brothers. He was able to look back on his life and see how God was preparing the way for the people of God to withstand the great famine that came on the land.

Joseph saw that he was part of the plan. He became Pharaoh's chief administrator, who provided the needed food for God's people during the famine. Joseph also recognized God's presence in his life, even when things were not going well for him as Joseph clung to the overwhelming and steadfast love of God. The struggles of his life transformed Joseph from a mistreated child into a compassionate and forgiving man.

Now, back to our question, **"How can we make bold moves towards the plan that God has for our lives?"**

And in our response, we might be like Joseph and make bold moves to forgive one another by letting go of our pain or resentment. And to boldly move forward, like Jesus, in God's love.

But forgiveness is not an easy process. Sometimes, we find ourselves saying, "I was not in the wrong; the other person was." But the scripture tells us to love anyhow. Jesus did no wrong but was nailed to the cross. Scriptures say they spit on his face. And after all that, he could still say, "Father, forgive them for they know not what they do." [51]

I know it is only human to wish something wrong happens to those who offended us. But, God is always present in brokenness. As Joseph was able to see God in their situation when he told his brothers, "God sent me, before you, to preserve life!" [52]

Forgiveness is not always easy, but 1 John 4:20, NIV, says, "If anyone says, I love God and hates their brothers and sisters, that person are liars: for those who do not love a brother or sister whom they have seen, cannot love God whom they have not seen."

Joseph exemplifies this merciful love after introducing himself to his brothers years after separating, as we learn that Joseph wept so loud that even the Egyptians heard it at a distance. Then he said to his brothers, "Come closer to me." [53] When the brothers came closer to Joseph, the 20 years of bitterness ended.

Like Joseph, we can try to invite those who might have offended us to get closer to us because they are probably afraid of how we may react. And so, we can be the ones to extend that invitation to get closer. That is why our church engages in educational discussions on racial belonging, LGBTQ+ belonging, gender belonging, cultural belonging, and religious belonging. Yes, these conversations are bold moves towards justice and peace, but we believe that the church of Jesus Christ calls upon us to be courageous people who embrace belonging!

As we see that belonging is needed, when the scripture tells us, that Joseph kissed all his brothers, and wept over them." But they already lost a lot of good years. No one could not get the years back, but Joseph made the most out of that moment and offered space for a new start.

In that, forgiveness teaches us about the valued treasures of restoring our love for God, ourselves, and one another by simply trusting in the plans that God has for our lives.

The importance of valued treasures is in a story about an angry man who ran through a Museum in Amsterdam and stopped when he reached Rembrandt's famous painting, "Night watch." While standing in front of the image, he took out a knife and slashed the painting repeatedly before anyone could stop him. A short time later, another distraught, hostile man slipped into St. Peter's Cathedral in Rome with a hammer and began to smash Michelangelo's beautiful sculpture, "The Pieta." [54]

And in those moments, two cherished works of art were severely damaged. But, the officials did not throw out these works of art! Instead, they used the best experts, who worked with the utmost care and precision to restore the treasures.

Forgiveness has the power to restore our brokenness. It can mend our relationships with ourselves, God, and one another. And this is the restoration song of today's psalmist, who hopes that one day, all the kindom, which is all of God's creation, could live together, in unity.

And so, let our prayers towards forgiveness draw us closer to God by trusting in the plan and purpose for us all. And let us also seek to restore our valuable relationships amongst humanity so that a watching world might learn of God's merciful love. May it be so. **AMEN.**

PRAYER

Compassionate God, we hear your voice calling for justice and peace amongst nations. And because of this, we ask that you bless our hospitality to strangers and enable our advocacy to transform us into being living examples of your loving Spirit in the name of Jesus Christ. **Amen.**

Be Transformed

What does it take to be transformed by God's love?

Sunday, August 23, 2020
Twelfth Sunday after Pentecost

Be Transformed

Today, we hear about the story of the infant Moses and how his life caused others to be, transformed. The Spirit of God revealed that Moses had something special about him, which caused his mother, sister, and Pharaoh's daughter, to save him, even at significant risks to themselves.

As we might ask, **"What does it take to be transformed by God's love?"**

Looking at scripture suggests that when we 1) seek to live into God's plan for our lives, we can 2) transform our fearful thoughts into acts of God's love.

God's purpose and plan are exampled in Moses' life today because, before the birth of Moses, the previous Egyptian Pharaoh favored Joseph, who was an Israelite by birth. Joseph forgave his brothers for trading him into slavery. And because of this, it was okay for Joseph's brothers and their relatives to enter Egypt. Thus, surviving the famine in their land during that time. And because they came into Egypt, the people of Israel flourished.

But, we learn in today's passage that the Pharaoh who favors Joseph dies. As time passes, more and more Pharaohs come and go until there is a Pharaoh who comes along to rule over Egypt, and this new Pharaoh did not know of the great things Joseph did for the nation of Egypt. This new Pharaoh only saw the flourishing Hebrews' threat to his kingdom.

This Pharaoh's fear led him to feel that because the Hebrews had done so well in Egypt, they might team up with the enemies of Egypt to overturn the nation and defeat the Egyptians. And with these thoughts in mind, this convinced the new Pharaoh that he must do something. So, he forced the Hebrews into slavery and later called for the death of all their boys.

It was during this time that Moses was born. And, God speaks, [55] over and above this unjust Pharaoh. It becomes evident that the midwives spare baby Moses' life. It also appears that God is leading Moses' mother to keep him in hiding for three months. And it seems that God is instructing Pharaoh's daughter to raise Moses as her son.

This story of the infant Moses, examples for us women, who appear to be without power and voice, respond to the voice of God, which empowers and guides each of them. And in doing so, God's guiding Spirit transforms them from being afraid of dismantling the systemic injustices that impacted a population of babies into being courageous and compassionate in doing what was right and just, for the sake of all, children.

Let us, now, return to our question, **"What does it take to be transformed by God's love?"**

It seems that we are to open our hearts to allow God to guide our lives and transform us from feeling voiceless and powerless into being courageous and compassionate children of God.

Overcoming our fears is shared in a story about a mother putting her four-year-old daughter to bed for the night. But, the child is afraid of the dark. And the mother, on this occasion, with her spouse away, is fearful, also. So, when the mother turns the light out, the child catches a glimpse of the moon outside the window. And she asks, "Mommy, is the moon God's light?" And her mom says, "Yes."

Then, the child asks, "Will God put out the moonlight and go to sleep?" And the mother replies, "No, dear, God never goes to sleep." Then, out of the simplicity of a child's faith, the little girl said something, which even gave reassurance to her mother. Saying, "Well, as long as God is awake, there is no sense, in both of us, staying awake." And off to sleep, she went. [56]

This story reminds us that when we have nothing left but God, then, for the first time, we become aware that God is enough. And, at this moment, we become transformed!

And that is why Paul's letter to the Romans today offers a firm theological foundation for resisting all unjust systems of domination by insisting we only conform to the will of God, which is good and acceptable and perfect. Paul reminds the church not to be conformed to the world but to be transformed by renewing our minds!! As we are to love one another, as God loves us all.

So, let us think about how God is speaking to us during this long summer with the COVID-19 virus. Let us think about all we are going through as the beloved community of God as we have so many of our loved ones who are sick. We have many of our loved ones struggling financially with rising debts. We see communities of color disproportionately adversely impacted by the virus. Even our grieving over the loss of loved ones affects us because of not gathering in person. And yet, God's voice is heard.

We know that God is still speaking because, while the virus has led to a 10% unemployment rate, so many more of us are working and capable of giving more so that all might be able to put food on our family's table. And while people are contracting the virus at alarming levels, especially here in South Florida, the rest of us can be good neighbors by wearing masks, sanitizing, and safe distancing to help reduce the fast spread of this virus.

Because, when we respond to God's calling for justice, we can be like those women in the early years of Moses' life, who showed God's loving compassion for all children. In that, we see that God has made provisions for everyone to have what we need and more.

As God is with us along our life's journey, and that is why the psalmist says, today, that 'our help, is in the name, of God!' [57] And when we reflect during this long summer and in every other moment of our lives, we can give thanks to God for being with us every step of the way.

Therefore, the psalmist offers a bold thanksgiving to God by acknowledging the injustice placed against a people by an unjust Pharaoh, who led in fear as the psalmist gives thanks for God's work in bringing liberation to the people by calling upon the women to act.

Even today, we have neighbors responding in fear rather than in love. We know of four white nationalist hate groups who are active right here in the West Palm Beach area. Their beliefs preach hate, division, and fear rather than offer a way of justice, compassion, and love.

But, even amid hate-mongering, we will hear the voice of God. In a true story about a young man who went to college, we listen to the voice of God when his classmates were surprised to find out he grew up in a hate group. And so, a Jewish classmate decided to invite him for dinner. Initially, the young white nationalist declined. But, the Jewish student asked again, and the white supremacist student accepted the invitation.

And because of that dinner, he changed his views on hate and transformed! [58]

And as a result, this young man is no longer a member of the white nationalist movement that preaches hate towards persons of color, same-gender-loving persons, and non-Christians. As we see, once again, that God's love rises above hate!!

But, while that story is powerful, I must admit that my favorite transformation story of all is about a young carpenter who lays aside his father's tools to take up the call of an itinerant preacher. And in doing so, for three years, he travels the hills and valleys of his native home.

And even though thousands would begin to follow him. Most of them would leave him because the local religious and political powers started to fear his power, which threatened theirs. With the growing fears of those in power, He is arrested by the local authorities, tortured, and put to death, like a common criminal.

Oh, but three days later, the story continues. Jesus is seen alive by his closest companions. Oh, how I love to tell that story. The story of Jesus Christ. As His life and death fulfill the plan of God to grant grace and mercy to sinners. In that, God's loving grace transforms life and is freely available, for us, all.

So, then, let us prayerfully continue to stand on the unfolding promises of God. Let us open our hearts to hear the voice of God's guiding Spirit, which helps us to overcome our fears. Let us place our cares and concerns into the hands of God, who has the power to transform our hearts and minds from hateful acts that divide into loving actions that unite. So, that we hear God tell us, 'well done, my good and faithful servant.' [59] May it be so. **AMEN.**

PRAYER

Living God, burn in us a deep understanding of the ways you move through words, through others, and us. May we be open to you and the things you are stirring in us. **Amen.**

LETTER TWENTY

Spirit-led Living

How might God's Spirit lead us to harmonious living?

<u>Sunday, August 30, 2020</u>
<u>Thirteenth Sunday after Pentecost</u>

Spirit-Led Living
Today, we hear about the spirit-led living that Paul mentions to the early Christians so that they could live in harmony.

As we ask, **"How might God's Spirit lead us to harmonious living?"**

The scripture suggests that when <u>we love God sincerely, we exercise care towards one another by our acts of humility.</u>

Since we recognize the kids this Sunday, the following thoughts from kids' views on love are interesting.
- I know my older sister loves me because she gives me all her old clothes and must go out and buy new ones.
- I let my big sister pick on me because my mom says she only likes me because she loves me. So, I pick on my baby sister because I love her.
- Love cards like Valentine's cards say stuff on them that we'd like to say ourselves, but we wouldn't be caught dead saying." [60]

But one of the things that the scripture deals with today is loving people who may be a bit more challenging to love.

For example, late one summer evening in Nebraska, a weary truck driver pulled his rig into an all-night truck stop. The waitress had just served him when three tough-looking motorcyclists decided to give him a hard time. Not only did they verbally abuse him, one grabbed the hamburger off his plate, but another also took a handful of his French fries, and the third picked up his coffee and began to drink it.

How do you think he responded? He calmly got up, picked up the check, walked to the front of the room, put the bill and his money on the cash register, and went out the door. The waitress followed him to put the money away and stood watching out the door as the big truck drove away into the night.

When she returned, one of the bikers said to her, "Well, he's not much of a man, is he?" She replied, "I don't know about that, but he sure ain't much of a truck driver. He just ran over three motorcycles on his way out of the parking lot." [61]

Many of us may understand how this truck driver feels. It is hard to be nice to some people. The gospel teaches us that we have an obligation to everyone, not just pleasant people. In today's scripture, Jesus instructs his disciples on having a healthy relationship with God's way.

Let's begin by learning a general principle that applies to every situation dealing with people. We can find this principle taught in many places, but we will first look at Romans, saying, "Do not be overcome by evil, but overcome evil with good." [62]

Here, we are asked not to do bad things to others when they do bad things because if we do, we become just like them. We have allowed them to control what we do. We have allowed their bad behavior to conquer us and make us respond incorrectly. We have been "overcome by evil."

Let me give an example that might appeal to our youth. In the movie "Star Wars," [63] the Emperor and Darth Vader are evil. They do bad things. Luke Skywalker is a good person. But, the Emperor and Darth Vader start doing bad things to Luke and his friends.

They want Luke to get angry and hateful so that Luke will become just like the - evil. They want Luke to join the Dark Side. If Luke lets the Emperor and Darth Vader make him 'return evil for evil,' they have beaten Luke. Luke has been "overcome by evil."

Instead of being "overcome by evil," Paul says we should "overcome evil with good." [64] That means we don't allow the bad things that people do to us, to make us do wrong, but we fight against it by being good.

Now, back to our question, **"How might God's Spirit lead us to harmonious living?"**

And our response can be striving to love God and one another faithfully, with prayerful humility. Because if we are not prayerful, "Pride can be the ground in which all other sins grow." [65]

For example, in his book, The Winner Within, [66] Basketball coach Pat Riley tells about the 1980 World Championship Los Angeles Lakers. They won the NBA Championship that year and were recognized as the best basketball team in the world. They began their 1980-81 season considered likely to win back-to-back championships. But within weeks of the season opener, Magic Johnson tore a cartilage in his knee and would be out for three months. The team and the fans rallied, and the remaining players played their hearts out. They determined to make it through that period without losing their rankings. They were winning seventy percent of their games when the time began to draw near for Magic Johnson to return to action.

As his return grew closer, the publicity surrounding him increased. During timeouts at the games, the public address announcer would always say, "And don't forget to mark your calendars from February 27. Magic Johnson returns to the lineup of your World Champion Los Angeles Lakers!"

During that announcement, the other players would complain, "What's so great about February 27? We're winning now." As the day approached, fewer and fewer things were written or said about the players putting out so much effort. Finally, the 27th came, and as they clicked through the turnstiles, every one of the 17,500 ticket holders were handed a button that said, "The Magic Is Back!" At least fifty press photographers crowded onto the floor while the players were introduced. Usually, only the starters were introduced, and Magic Johnson would be on the bench when the game began. But he was nevertheless included in the introductions. At the mention of his name, the arena rocked with a standing ovation. Flashbulbs went off like popcorn. Magic Johnson was like a retuning god to the crowd that night.

Meanwhile, the other players who had carried the team for three months and were ignored were seething with jealousy, resentment, anger, and envy. They were so resentful that they barely won the game that night against one of the worst teams in the league. Eventually, the morale of the entire team collapsed. The players turned on each other. The coach was fired. And they ultimately lost in the first round of the playoffs.

Riley said, "Because of greed, pettiness, and resentment, we executed one of the fastest falls from grace in NBA history. It was the Disease of Me."

Yet, Paul is encouraging the church to live harmoniously, set our pride aside, and work together, as the Body of Christ humbly, serving together, as one.

Like the story of helping a hurt friend cross the finish line at the Special Olympics. Amazing!

Friends, we all have our ideas about love, but the love that comes from God is the greatest love of all. As someone once said: A bell is not a bell until you ring it; A song is not a song until you sing it, and love in your heart is not love until you give it away.

May the Spirit of God continuously lead us into loving relationships with one another. **Amen.**

PRAYER

Loving God, in whom we move and have our being, tune our lives to experience your wonder and mystery. **Amen.**

LETTER TWENTY-ONE

Remember, Restore, Renew

How might remembering God's faithfulness restore and renew us today?

<u>Sunday, September 6, 2020</u>
<u>Fourteenth Sunday after Pentecost</u>

Remember, Restore, Renew
On this Communion Sunday, the scripture calls upon believers to **remember, restore, and renew** their faith in God.

As we can ask, **"How might remembering God's faithfulness restore and renew us today?**

In looking at the scripture, it suggests that we <u>first remember God's loving acts </u>so that we might<u> be able to help restore and renew the world that God loves.</u>

Remembering, restoring, and renewing how we are to love one another is at the heart of our message for today—as we hear a great example of this kind of love, told by Archbishop Desmond Tutu of South Africa. Bishop Tutu says, 'that when he was a young boy, he had a life-changing experience.

He says that 'in South Africa, at that time, if a black person and a white person met while walking on a path, the black person was expected to get off the path and allow the white person to pass by. As they were passing by, the black person was supposed to nod their head as a gesture of respect." [67]

Then, Bishop Tutu says, 'one day, he and his mother were walking down the street when they noticed a tall white man, dressed in a black suit, walking towards them. And before he and his mother could step off the sidewalk, this man stepped off and allowed him and his mother to pass by. And as they passed by, the man tipped his hat, in a gesture of respect, to his mother."

Bishop Tutu recalls being a shocked kid who asked his mother, 'Why did the white man do that?' And his mother explained that the white man was an Anglican Priest. A man of God, which is why he did what he had done. And Bishop Tutu would later say, 'I decided there and then, that I wanted to be an Anglican Priest too.' But, more importantly, he said, 'I wanted to be a man of God.' This act of love is something that Bishop Tutu never forgot. Even as a child, it restored his hope in humanity. It renewed his faith in God throughout the years of his life. Because of his faithfulness in God, he was known for his justice and peace work as an anti-apartheid and human rights activist and became the first black African to hold the position.

God's message of love towards all people is in today's Exodus passage. In that, we see God speaking to Moses and his brother, Aaron, and telling them that their people are to remember and celebrate their freedom from slavery in Egypt when God allowed their children to be passed over from the deadly plague.

As God's message of love is a clarion call for people to see the importance of treating others, the way they will treat themselves. Because the children of Egypt were treated in the same manner that they treated the children of Israel. In that, the Exodus story begs us to remember that no matter how powerful a person, or some entity, feels that they are, God's love and almighty power remains transformative and supreme.

Now back to our question, **"How might remembering God's faithfulness restore and renew us today?**

Paul's letter today reminds us that, 'Love does no harm to a neighbor.' [68] If we remember this teaching, we become more humbled. And the more humbled we become, the more love we will have to give. Because humility is not only concerned with restoring and renewing oneself, it is about offering care and compassion to everyone.

And Jesus examples this type of loving humility when He spoke to His disciples about what true greatness looks like and says, "You know that the rulers of the Gentiles lord it over them, and their high officials exercise authority over them. Not so with you. Instead, whoever wants to become great among you must be your servant, and whoever wants to be first, must be your servant just as the Son of Man did not come to be served, but to serve, and to give his life, as a ransom for many." [69]

As we remember that Jesus exampled this kind of loving service when He fed the hungry, took care of the sick, loved the sinners, spent time with the outcasts, the lepers, and all of those on the margins of society. Jesus got to know all kinds of people. And in doing so, He restored them and renewed their lives. And as people of faith, we are asked to go and do the same.

In that, each worker, judge or janitor, sales clerk or scientist, mother, or millionaire CEO is equal in the sight of God, and each one has value and dignity. And, through our humility, we can see that being God's love in the world means that we know the image of God in everyone. And when we do, our acts of love will offer more fulfillment than our owning mansions, cars, boats, or having lots of money. Because Jesus teaches us that the true path towards completion, in this life, comes through giving ourselves away, in service to others, ask one of the volunteers at our food pantry!!

Humility reminds us that loving acts are at the heart of caring for all people. It creates in us something bigger than ourselves. It allows us to live into God's purpose and plan, not only for our lives but for the lives of us all. Like Bishop Tutu, the Israelites, the Gentiles, and all who seek systems of equality, it is heartening to see people of different races, neighborhoods, and faith traditions coming together to change the trajectory of the narrative of America's treatment of blacks and the poor.

As we can suspect, like when Bishop Tutu was a kid, observing the world around him, our children and grandchildren, nieces and nephews, are watching us, too—taking notice of what we are doing and what we are not, doing wondering how God, fits, into it all.

And when they ask, we can tell the children that we seek to be like Jesus. We can do so by showing love towards everyone while we are on earth to best prepare ourselves for the way it will be in heaven because we believe that when we get to heaven, there will not be a section for whites and a section for blacks. We think that when we get to heaven, there will not be a section for the poor and a section for the rich. We believe that when we get to heaven, there will not be a section for the LGBTQ+ and those who were not. We think that when we get to heaven, there will not be a section for those who spoke English and those who did not. We believe that when we ALL get to heaven, there will be a time of rejoicing. Because we will be with our loved ones, our ancestors, along with our angels who we feel have kept us from harm, and most of all, we will be with our loving, and merciful, God!!

Because of our response to the children, maybe it will inspire them to go and make a difference in the lives of neighbors, near and far. So, they, too, can grow into being the kinds of adults, like Jesus, Bishop Tutu, and the church universal by continuing to help make a difference in the ways that we treat one another here on earth.

And to remind us of God's love, today's Psalm says, 'Sing unto God, a new song' [70] because 'God delights in the humble and crowns them with victory.' [71] As this psalmist reminds us, God is within us, and that God's presence is all around us restoring us from all, that causes us to feel empty or sad and renewing us into the purpose, and the plan… that God has for us all!!

And so, let us remember all the people who came before us, who served faithfully and humbly so that we can be here today in our diversity. Let us restore our faith with the humility of Jesus, who taught us to care for all the beloved community. And, let us continue to renew ourselves by drawing closer to God, striving for a world whereby every person is afforded decency, justice, and fair treatment. May it be so. **AMEN.**

PRAYER

Loving God, you call us to embrace both you and the children of this world with unconditional love. Give us the grace to discern what you demand of us so that we may serve you faithfully, with an open heart. **Amen.**

Road to Freedom

Are we willing to be on the road to freedom?

<u>Sunday, September 13, 2020</u>
<u>Fifteenth Sunday after Pentecost</u>

Road to Freedom
Today, we hear potent examples about a road to freedom for the early believers, which calls upon them to put their faith in God humbly.

And as we hear this message, let us ask, "**Are we willing to be on the road to freedom today?**"

In looking at the scripture, it suggests that we <u>first humbly trust in God's faithfulness so that we secondly follow in the ways of God's love, which guides us still.</u>

In this familiar story about Moses and the people of Israel crossing the Red Sea, we see that God allows a pathway to freedom in an army against them.

A road to freedom is not always easy, as we can imagine how those Israelites felt, fleeing Pharaoh and following Moses while standing at the edge of the sea. They must have wondered how they were going to get across it.

And then, they see Moses, under God's guidance, would part the waters with his staff. And under their feet, the ground was dry, but on the other side, large waves of water looked ready to come down upon them.

As this road to freedom is not without danger ask a refugee, a soldier, or one of the Freedom Riders in the American south, in 1961. [72]

Two Freedom Riders responded to this question; the man known as getting into 'good trouble,' [73] John Lewis, who would become a U.S. Congressman, and Jim Zwerg, a UCC minister. The Freedom Riders were trained in nonviolence and rode buses throughout the south, promoting integration. And that is how they got their name, 'Freedom Riders.' But, those rides could be life-threatening. And this was so, on May 20, 1961, when a bus originating in Nashville pulled into a Montgomery Greyhound station. Men were waiting and hiding and armed with baseball bats, ready to inflict pain. Two of their victims included John Lewis and Jim Zwerg. They were severely beaten and did not know if they would live through it. But, they did, and the incident was published in newspapers worldwide, and the world could see what happened to these non-violent Freedom Riders.

The Exodus story and the Freedom Riders show the road to freedom is not always safe, but it is a gift given to the present by those from the past. And, it is a gift we give to the future by what we do right now.

And so, let us return to our question, **"Are we willing to be on the road to freedom today?"**

If we consider ourselves Christian, then the answer is "YES!" Because we understand that while a road to freedom is not easy, we trust that God's love and faithfulness from years past are guiding us, still.

Paul's letter today offers a great example of how we are to live together in peace as diverse people of faith by giving glory to God. In that, Paul acknowledges we see things differently, but, even in our differences, we are to remain humble and kind towards one another. We give God the glory in our food and not criticize our different food preferences. This acknowledgment will keep us humbled and focused on God.

As Paul emphasizes, we should focus on our relationship with God. And in doing so, we will humble ourselves before God and follow in the ways of peace and justice for all people regardless of how different we might be. And a man by the name of Dietrich Bonhoeffer, a paramount leader in the church in Nazi Germany, believed in this kind of Christian love. And as a result, he was imprisoned and tortured because he disagreed with Hitler and did not teach hate in the church.

But, before he died, Bonhoeffer [74] wrote these words to his twin sister, Sabine:

"It is good to learn early enough that sadness and God are not a contradiction, but rather a unity... for the idea that God is suffering, is one that has always been one of the most effective teachings of Christianity. [As it seems at times] that God is nearer to us in our suffering, and to find God in this way, gives peace and rest, and a strong and courageous heart."

Bonhoeffer's letter was like Paul's letter. In that, it speaks of everyone having to bow before God. And when we understand that our relationship with God is strong, we know that there is hope for us. It means that we no longer wallow in a life of despair and isolation because we know of God's justice, joy, and peace. It means that while we may never be perfectly obedient, we can follow the path that Jesus Christ set forth for us, and that is to follow in the way of God's love.

The way to discover God's love is in the story about a small country church. And, on one Sunday, before the sermon, the pastor announced, "I'd like to introduce a guest minister who is with us today." The pastor went on to tell the congregation that the guest minister was a very close friend and that he wanted him to say a few words. So, the elderly man stepped up to the pulpit and said, "A father, a son, and a friend of his son, were sailing off the Pacific coast when a fast-moving storm blocked the way to get back to shore. Even though the father was an experienced sailor, the waves were so high that he could not keep the boat upright.

So, the ocean swept the three of them as the boat capsized. Grabbing a rescue line, the father had to make the most excruciating decision of his life. Which boy would he save with the lifeline? Would he throw the line to his son, whom he loved beyond comparison, or would he throw it to the other boy? And he only had seconds to make his decision because he knew that he, most likely, could not save them both.

The agony of his decision was overwhelming. "As the father yelled out, 'I love you, son!' he threw a lifeline to his son's friend. By the time the father had pulled the boy back to the capsized boat, his son had disappeared under the raging water. His body was never found." He continued, saying, "The father knew his son would step into eternity with Jesus. So, he sacrificed his son to save the son's friend." The elder minister paused and looked at the congregation.

Then, he said, "How great is the love of God that He should do the same for us. Our Heavenly Father sacrificed His only begotten Son so that we could be saved. If you do not yet know him, I urge you to accept His offer to rescue you and take hold of the lifeline He is throwing out to you today."

The pastor returned to the pulpit and gave a brief sermon, with an invitation at the end. But no one responded, and soon, the service ended,

Immediately, two teenagers were at the elderly man's side, saying politely, "That was a nice story, but I don't think it was very realistic." And the man replied, "Well, you've got a point there." Then a peaceful smile broke out on his narrow face as he looked at his worn bible.

"It sure isn't very realistic, is it? But, that story gives me a glimpse of what it must have been like for God to choose Jesus to give up His life so that we all could be saved. All in the name of hope. You see, I was that father, and your pastor is my son's friend." [75]

And that is why the scripture says, "if you shall be free in Jesus Christ, then you shall be free indeed." [76] Because, with Christ, we will be to love each other as we love ourselves. With Christ, we will be free to oppose hostile forces that teach us to fear and hate one another. With Christ, we will be free to hope for a better world by seeking paths towards peace. With Christ, we will be free to stand up for equal justice on behalf of everyone, everywhere. As freedom in Christ allows us to trust in God's mercy for all the beloved community.

But, if we get into 'good trouble' for freedom and become a little weary, we can quote this old saying, 'Must Jesus bear the cross alone, and all the world goes free. No. There is a cross for everyone, and there is a cross for me.' [77]

So, let us be thankful for the faithfulness that heals our wounded spirits and makes us whole again. And, let us trust in the almighty power of God so that together, we will continue to journey alongside each other on God's road to freedom. May it be so. **AMEN.**

PRAYER

God of peace, help us through every moment of the journey. **Amen.**

LETTER TWENTY-THREE

Tension in the Wilderness

How can we face tension and stress in the wilderness moments of life?

<u>Sunday, September 20, 2020</u>
<u>Sixteenth Sunday after Pentecost</u>

Tension in the Wilderness

On this Sunday, when we prepare to imagine our future together as a church, we read Paul's letter to the early church in Rome about God's future glory that is coming for all creation. Paul writes his hope for the church, even amid their stress and tension, and encourages them to find peace in the wilderness.

In today's brief sermon, we might ask, **"How can we face tension and stress in the wilderness moments of life?"**

In looking at the scripture, it simply suggests that no matter how difficult or even desperate our situation seems, Paul reminds us we can face it with hope. (Read Romans 8:18-25, NIV)

The example used in the scripture about birth pangs brought about mixed feelings for me. On the one hand, those moments of expecting our baby were blissful because he was our third child and the only one to go full term. But on the other hand, when the birth pangs got to be so great that I would groan, the nurses could not seem to give me enough meds as waiting for the birth to occur seemed longer and longer by the moment! But as Paul has written, the hope of what was to come helped me get through it.

But as we look around, beyond our personal life experiences, we don't have to be a very astute observer to notice that we live in a world that struggles with hopelessness. Many of us who engage in a conversation with others may tell us they are discouraged. When we listen to some radio talk shows or watch the news, we can hear people cynical about life and think the world is going down the tubes. And on a world scale, it seems that we go from crisis to crisis.

As Paul talks about life, he uses language that helps us see life as an eternal plan. We live here on earth for a little while, but God's plan is for us to have everlasting life. Paul wants to make sure that we don't get so discouraged with the difficulties of this life that we lose sight of the big picture of eternity. In that, he tells them that there will be a time when there won't be any more struggles, pain, death, or tears. And, those in Christ will know joy and happiness as the gift of hope that Paul points to is a tremendous benefit of knowing Jesus Christ as our Lord and Savior.

And because of our hope, we can turn our eyes away from being brought down by temporary pain and focus on the future of God's glory. This hope is a truth that Paul also expressed in 2 Corinthians 1:3-4, NIV, saying, 'Praise be to the God and Father of our Lord Jesus Christ, the Father of compassion and the God of all comfort, who comforts us in all our troubles, so that we can comfort those in any situation, with the comfort we have received from God as God is the comfort needed to have peace in our tensions in the wilderness, regardless of our concerns or struggles.' As God's comfort and peace deeps our faith in God and provides us with the spiritual medicine that helps us renew and sustain our hope.

And that is why Paul writes that the Spirit of God is within us and waiting for us to deliver or birth our growing love for God and one another. What a fantastic future God has in store for the church universal!

Now, let us return to our question, **"How can we face tension and stress in the wilderness moments of life,"** full of hope. Hopeful in the future glory that God has planned for all of creation. Optimistic in the waiting, the wandering, and the wondering of our earthly desires, knowing that God is working so that whatever we might be experiencing, all things are working together for our good because we love the Lord!

But as comforting as this scripture may feel when things are good, often when things are not going so well, one can ask how can suffering and hardship be for our good.

Yet, Paul addresses this question nicely as he finishes out this 8th chapter with words I believe are some of the most important words for everyone.

"There is nothing that can separate us from the love of God." [78] Nothing you can do can make God stop loving you and caring for you. No situation you can find yourself in will be a place where God's love cannot reach you. Not even death can triumph over God's love.

An example of this scripture was played out in the movie, The Shawshank Redemption, [79] as an innocent man finds himself spending 20 years in prison for a crime he didn't commit. It's a dark, lifeless, helpless place made of bars and stone. Prison - and there are all kinds - is a place where a person can give up on life itself. Listen to this beautiful short scene about hope between two friends, Andy and Red.

ANDY: Here's where it makes the most sense. We need it, so we don't forget.
RED: Forget?
ANDY: Forget that; there are places not made from stone in the world. There is something inside that they can't get to, that they can't touch; it's yours.
RED: What are you talking about?

135

ANDY: Hope.

Hope is what we have. The love of God is what we have, which reaches out to us no matter how distant we may seem or how desperate we may be.

It's like birth pangs as we all experience what can be considered stressful moments that feel like tensions in the wilderness. And in those times when we experience the pains of this world, we might often let out a groan, just as Paul mentions. Maybe it's when a friend, a child, a parent, or someone we love does something we wish they wouldn't have, or we know they shouldn't have. And out of frustration, we groan.

Maybe it's when circumstances arise that causes us or someone we love pain. And out of pity, we groan. But Paul says that groaning is a sign of our hope. We are longing for something better. And if we are in Christ, we have the promise that there is something better. So, as we groan, we remember our hope that someday things will be better. We have hope! And that hope for the future can and should affect our present outlook.

Let us remember throughout the journey that there will be tension in our lives, but may we also remember in those times that God's love is still with us, giving purpose and meaning to our lives. And the life of Christ affirms this hope for our future glory with the Lord as Jesus lived and suffered for us. But this was for our good because, after His earthly death, Jesus Christ rose again, showing the world not only of God's power but, more importantly, of God's love.

So, let us humble ourselves in our wilderness. Let us also wait in anticipation of God's loving purpose for our lives. And let us live with peace during every circumstance so that we might offer others the hope of God's everlasting love! **Amen.**

PRAYER

Loving God, help sustain us with your life-giving water vital for the journey and guide us to be used as your symbols of healing and hope in the world. **Amen.**

God's Sustaining Presence

How might God's presence sustain our lives?

<u>Sunday, September 27, 2020</u>
<u>Seventeenth Sunday after Pentecost</u>

God's Sustaining Presence
Today, we hear about the early believers who call upon **God's sustaining presence** to be with them. As we learn that those thirsty found your living water and those who were lost found your everlasting hope!!

And in hearing this, we can ask, **"How might God's presence sustain our lives today?"**

The scriptures call upon us to <u>first trust that God is with us on the journey so that we can secondly be guided and used as God's hope and love in the world.</u>

The Exodus story speaks about God's people journeying together and wondering why God would leave them thirsty in the desert. And, if we were to be completely honest, we, like those early believers, have also asked, at least once, whether God was still with us on the journey.

As we, as a church, are continuing to journey together towards a better way of life for all people. In that, we continue traveling together for those who lack food. We continue touring together for those who seek clean water. We continue journeying together for those who are crying out for equal justice. We continue traveling together on behalf of all who are longing for peace in neighborhoods, everywhere!!

And so, let us imagine for a moment, imagine how the people of Israel must have felt, journeying together, in the desert, with no water in sight. And, like anyone who thirsts, they began to complain. They also got angry. And, they questioned whether God was present with them.

And so, in their frustration, they began to argue and complain to Moses.

But, like any good leader, Moses, calls out to God for help!! And God guides Moses to the place where there is enough water, for all, to drink!!!

God's sustaining presence is also in today's letter to the Philippians. As Paul's letter reminds the early believers in Philippi, Jesus Christ is our living example of God's hope and love in all our lives.

Paul's message can be paraphrased in the famous saying that youth started in the late 1980s, "What Would Jesus Do?" As Paul addresses the community's conflict over their differences by basically telling them, "What Jesus WOULD Do." As Paul goes on to remind them, Jesus would say to them to love one another, even in their differences.

Then, Paul explains HOW they are to love one other by telling them, "What Jesus WOULD Do." As Paul goes on to remind them, when we see someone in need, we are to reach out and, like Jesus, lend a helping hand.

But, Paul does not stop there. Paul reminds them that if Jesus Christ humbled himself to become human, then we, regardless of who we are, should not think that we are better than anyone else. Paul emphasizes that Jesus Christ became human, so we all might know that God equally loves us in humble obedience to God.

Paul closes his letter, reminding the believers to reverence God, not to him. And for them to place their energy in the hope and love that God has given to them all.

Now, let us return to our question, **"How might God's presence sustain our lives today?"**

God's presence can sustain us when we choose to adopt an attitude of Jesus Christ!!

Because, by following in the ways of Jesus, we can live harmoniously, as the beloved community. But, in a world that can be so mean. Our choosing to adopt an attitude of Jesus Christ offers hope to a hurting world. It offers hope beyond the heaviness of our hearts, especially in those times when we are doing our best, and our best still does not seem to be enough.

Adopting an attitude of Jesus Christ gives us hope, even when the beloved community is at war amongst itself, and it seems that peace is in a far distance.

Adopting an attitude of Jesus Christ gives us hope, even when the beloved community divides into red states and blue states, and someone calls another evil, subhuman, or no longer my friend!!!

Adopting an attitude of Jesus Christ gives us hope, even when the beloved community experiences continuing systemic racism, sexism, classism, and so many more –isms that bring about separation!

Adopting an attitude of Jesus Christ gives us hope, even when the beloved community bullies one another at school, at work, on the highway, in homes, or yes, even at church.

It is important to note that Paul wrote this letter so that those believers would remember God's sustaining presence, even while imprisoned and facing death.

Moses called out to God in the desert on behalf of the people who were thirsting for water and near death so that they, too, would be reminded of God's sustaining presence in their time of need.

Both the Philippians, and the people of Israel, were groups of people, who were like you, and me. They were a beloved community, grappling with what it means to trust in God. Both Moses and Paul undoubtedly trusted in God; they were both concerned with the selfishness and arrogance of the believers. And they knew that their greed and arrogance threatened the love, unity, and fellowship of the beloved community.

As one scholar writes, "There is no room for a feel-good religion that does not take its servant role seriously. There is no room for a victory that does not first know the 'fellowship of his sufferings on behalf of others; no room for righteousness that does not pour out... yes, even empty, oneself for the interests of others." [80]

As we see, being God's hope and love in the world is a dire and powerful message!! And it is impressive that a group of youth who created the "WWJD?" wristbands embraced this critical question for all who identify as Christians.

As the notable theologian, Dietrich Bonhoeffer wrote, "The church, is the church, only when, it exists for others especially, since "We live in a world dominated by anger, and the attitude of 'me first." [81]

Because, instead of loving those who persecute us, we throw bombs. Instead of forgiving, we hold a grudge, and as a result, we give little room for grace and have little flexibility for human error. And this makes little room for love to flood in and take over.

But, as the Body of Christ, we are called to focus on Christian humility, unity, and fellowship. We are to love others with loving actions. We are to have an attitude of Christ-like humility that does not hold a grudge, and that does not say, "My way or the highway!" Because when we have the attitude of Christ, we seek to love everyone.

And so, let us imagine what this world can be if every moment of every day we pray to God, asking that all the beloved community adopt the attitude of Christ.

Let us imagine a time when those who come across our paths will know that we are Christians by our acts of love towards everyone, everywhere.

And let us imagine ourselves being changed, moved, and molded into being better by God's sustaining presence, waking us up from our sleep so that when we open our eyes to the cries of justice and peace for all, we will never be the same. May it be so. **Amen.**

PRAYER

Spirit of the Living God stirs within us a deep understanding of the ways you move through words, through others, and us so that we may be the people who help cultivate kindness and hope for the journey. **Amen.**

LETTER TWENTY-FIVE

Wisdom for the Way

What is God's wisdom calling upon us to do?

Sunday, October 4, 2020
Eighteenth Sunday after Pentecost

Wisdom for the Way
Today, the scriptures teach early believers that it is wise to follow God!

And as believers, ourselves, we can ask, **"What is God's wisdom calling upon us to do?"**

The scriptures suggest that first, we seek to deepen our understanding of God so that, secondly, we live out what it means to love our neighbor as we love ourselves.

In the Exodus story, we see the dramatic entrance of thunder and lightning, reminding the people of Israel to give reverence to God the One, who brought them out from slavery, the One who has been with them throughout the generations, and the One, who is with them still.

God calls upon the beloved community to take seriously losing their moral compass. And that is why we see that God gets their attention. In that, God gets them to stop and pay attention to how they are living out their lives as God's call gets them to take seriously the wisdom that comes from being caring and compassionate neighbors and as people of God.

These words of wisdom are famously known as the ten commandments. And these words have become the foundation for the greatest commandment of all, in which Jesus Christ tells us that 'we are to love God, and to love our neighbors as we love ourselves.' [82] Love is exampled in each command, which says…
1- No other gods; 2- no graven image; 3- not taking God's name in vain; 4- honoring the Sabbath; 5- honoring your parents; 6- no killing; 7- no adultery; 8- no stealing; 9- no lying on your neighbor; and 10- not wanting to take what your neighbor has. [83]

Each command is all about how we can better love God, ourselves, and how to love our neighbor as we love ourselves!!

As Paul's letter, today examples this kind of love shown through Jesus Christ. As Paul writes that to know Christ is to be like Christ, and because of this, they should fill the air with Christ's praise as they move forward, together, as the beloved community.

And to further illustrate what he means, Paul considers himself in a race but not just any kind of race. As Paul's race was the life he was living.

Paul did what we are supposed to do when we are about to run the most critical race of our lives. He considered all his resources and requirements and considered all the rewards.

Paul's life reflects what it takes to run a race. From scripture, we can gather that Paul came from a highly regarded Jewish family history. He furthered his success by adding years of education, social climbing, and exhausting work so that he could be among the best and ahead of everyone else. But then, one day, Paul encountered, first-hand, the love of Jesus Christ. And it was in those moments Paul realized that while he was racing, he noticed that he was running fast, in the wrong direction!

God showed Paul that there was still a race to run. Paul was to suit up for a different team. And by doing so, Paul changed, and he stopped causing harm to the Christians that he had persecuted for years. And instead, Paul became a Christian. Because Paul changed, instead of feeling superior to those who were less educated, he had become a teacher who shared the loving ways of Jesus Christ with anyone, anywhere. And, because Paul changed, instead of thinking that his understanding of God's love was only limited to a select community, Paul now realized that through Jesus Christ, God's love is equally shared, amongst all people, everywhere. As Paul was once racing fast, in the wrong direction, but because of his encounter with Jesus Christ, Paul made an about-face and spread the Word of God's love, which stayed with him until Paul, finished his race!

Now, let us return to our question, **"What is God's wisdom calling upon us to do?"**

We can look to God's loving wisdom, which is calling upon each of us to 'keep the faith' and follow in the way of kindness even amongst those who are the most difficult of neighbors. And when we follow a moral compass, God will lead us down the right paths.

God's unconditional love and wisdom are here to guide us along the journey so that we can continue pressing toward the goal that God has for each of our lives.

As a church, we continue pressing toward justice and peace. We will not need a food pantry one day because our society would have created a justice system, whereby everyone would have the food they need to feed themselves and their family.

We continue pressing forward toward a goal of justice and peace. One day, we will not need to provide shelter for those families without a home because our society would have created a justice system where everyone would have a safe refuge called home.

We continue pressing forward toward a goal of justice and peace so that one day we will not need to say that 'Black Lives Matter,' [84] because

All Lives Will Matter. Our society would have created a justice system whereby everyone would be treated equitably in their homes, in their neighborhoods, on their jobs, and yes, in the church. And to make sure that all know they are welcome in this church, we have declared ourselves an Anti-Racist Church.

Because, as a church, we are continuing to press towards the high calling of Jesus Christ, who calls upon us to love everyone, from every place, as equal citizens of God's creation.

As there are more than enough resources for all to have the basic needs of life, our Christian response is to follow in the way of Jesus Christ and work to help eliminate all the many disparities. But, Moses, Jesus, and Paul teach that we can be a harmonious community, moving forward when we allow God's wisdom to lead the way.

Like today's psalmist, we can also pray that our ways might be pleasing and acceptable to God, who is our rock and our redeemer. In that, we all need to be encouraged from time to time so that we can KEEP THE FAITH! Especially in times like these, when we are all impacted, somehow or another. Some of us are grappling with health concerns; some are dealing with financial problems; some are dealing with domestic situations. And some of us are planning a substantial post-COVID-19 party. Honestly, it is a thing!

And to emphasize this point, of having the wisdom to remain faithful in every season of life, there is a person that I like to quote, who is one of the most famous English historical figures. Winston Churchill. He simply said three words and then left the podium. 'Never give up.'

And so, let us remain hopeful in God's wisdom as exampled in the life of Jesus Christ, who shows us what it means to love justice and kindness. This time of change may change us and draw us closer to God, who reveals to us that there is only one actual race: the human race. May it be so. **AMEN.**

PRAYER

Living God, we pray for a deeper understanding of the ways you move through us. May we continuously celebrate Your goodness in every way. **Amen.**

Praiseworthy Living

What does it mean for us to offer praiseworthy living?

<u>Sunday, October 11, 2020</u>
<u>Nineteenth Sunday after Pentecost</u>

Praiseworthy Living
Today, we hear God's call for people of faith to have praiseworthy living, no matter what their circumstances might be!

And in reflection, we might ask, **"What does it mean for us to offer praiseworthy living?"**

Paul's letter suggests that praiseworthy living can occur when <u>we celebrate God in our daily prayers, which helps us to replace our worries with God's peace.</u>

We hear a great example of how we praise God in all things from today's psalmist, who says that we are to praise God because God is good, and God's steadfast love endures forever.

And we see this kind of praiseworthy living from Paul, in verse 6, when he writes, "Don't worry about anything." [85] But, not worrying, this seems nearly impossible… even for people of faith.

Suppose we were to use ourselves as an example. In that case, we could feel validated in our worrying, especially as we continue to face significant life adjustments that have impacted us all somehow due to the COVID-19 virus, along with the injustices that challenge us every day.

But, worrying is not unique to our unprecedented year of 2020. Research from the Mayo Clinic in recent years claims that 80-85% of its total caseload has been due directly to worry and anxiety, as many experts say that coping with stress is a top health priority.

The Medical science field sees that worrying is closely tied to heart trouble, blood pressure problems, ulcers, thyroid malfunction, migraine headaches, and a host of stomach disorders.

For example, around 25 million Americans have high blood pressure due to stress or anxiety, 8 million have stomach ulcers, and every week 112 million people take medication for stress-related symptoms.

But, how can we NOT worry? And this could have been the question of the early believers, too!

But, Paul was no stranger to difficult times.

After all, Paul continued to praise God, even though he was in jail awaiting his trial. As 2 Cor 11 gives us the details of Paul's challenging days. We learn that they beat and stoned him, put him in constant danger, and he even faced financial stress, which caused him to go hungry at times. Paul indeed has the credibility to speak about worry.

But, to understand more fully what Paul meant by worrying is to translate it into Greek, which tells us that worrying is to have a divided mind between the worries of the world and the peace of God.

One of the ways Paul examples this kind of praiseworthy living of not worrying is by learning that he has limitations as Paul realized that he had done all he could do. And, now, he had to put his trust in God.

So, this message tells us that even if we feel like we are near rock bottom, it is not too late to turn our focus to God. And when we lean on God, we feel the love of Jesus Christ, who is with us, through every trial and is the kind of friend who is present to keep us from despair. Paul mentions in verse 2 that he will continue praising God because of God's love and presence.

As Paul examples his faith when he says, in verse 8, "We are hard-pressed, from every side but, not crushed." [86] The hard times that Paul refers to are the times when we cannot see the bigger picture and ask WHY God would allow us to lose our job or when we ask WHY God would allow us to get sick or when we ask WHY God would allow us to lose our loved ones before we were ready for them to leave us.

As Paul reminds the believers, while we are hard-pressed on every side, we are not struck down or crushed because God is our help!

Bringing us back to our question, **"What does it mean for us to offer praiseworthy living?"**

Praiseworthy living calls upon us to seek God in all things. And to do so by praying and trusting in the plans that God has for our lives. We heard Moses deliver this message to the early believers when they began to worry and strayed away from God as we see that they began to worry because they failed to pray.

And that is why we will pause for the next two Monday evenings, to pray, with, and for our nation. We will pray for our collective grief for all the suffering caused by the lives lost during the pandemic, and we will pray that by God's grace, our nation will come together and begin to heal.

As Paul says, "Be anxious for nothing but in everything by prayer and supplication, with thanksgiving, [87] let our requests be made known to God. He doesn't just say, "Pray about it"; rather, he uses words to describe how to respond to the worry and anxiety we face. As Paul suggests, "Do not worry about anything, but in everything by prayer and supplication with thanksgiving let your requests be made known to God." [88]

Sheila Harvey

"By Prayer," making our requests known to God through the idea of adoration, devotion, and worship is essential. Whenever we find ourselves worrying, our first action can be to get alone with God and pray. To rejoice in God's nearness of God's goodness, as exampled through Jesus Christ whose love is more significant than any worry and whose peace surpasses all understanding which examples for us all, praiseworthy living.

And this is the kind of praiseworthy living that was lived out loud yesterday, during our conference-wide zoom annual gathering. A resolution was brought before all the churches of the Florida Conference, asking that we vote on "Becoming an Anti-Racist Church." [89] The resolution names the challenges that our broader society is grappling with; our response is to seek to be the welcoming church, whereby all will feel safe to worship, here, and know they belong, regardless of their racial make-up.

And it was heartening to witness that everyone who cast their vote was unanimous, in favor of the resolution for the Florida Conference of the United Church of Christ, to proudly declare that we are an Anti-Racist Church, where all are welcome and belong.

And so, let us continue to give God our best, and may our efforts grant us peace. Let us also trust God, whose love is more significant than our worry. And, let us take everything to God in prayer, knowing that God is good. Let it be so. **Amen.**

PRAYER

Spirit of the Living God, stir within us a deep understanding of the ways you move through words, through others, and us so that we may be the people who help cultivate kindness and hope for the journey. **Amen.**

LETTER TWENTY-SEVEN

Living Messages

How can our faith reveal that God's mercy still exists among us today?

<u>Sunday, October 18, 2020</u>
<u>Twentieth Sunday after Pentecost</u>

Living Messages
Today, we read how Moses and Paul become the living messages which remind the early believers that God will set all people free from their brokenness. Because no one is perfect, but God's loving mercy redeems us.

As we might ask, **"How can our faith reveal that God's mercy is still living among us today?"**

As the scripture seems to suggest that if we <u>remember God's faithful love for us all, then our lives can serve as a living witness to God's goodness and mercy.</u>

And in Paul's letter, we hear him reminding those early Christians about God's faithfulness and encouraging them to be 'imitators' or examples, of God's goodness, in every season.

But, the best way to understand why Paul had to write a letter, instead of being with them in person, is to paint a big picture of what was happening when he wrote the letter to the church in Thessalonica. And here is the reason why.

When Paul wrote the letter, about 200,000 people lived in Thessalonica, and most were Greeks, but there were also many Romans and a substantial Jewish minority.

And in Acts chapter 17, Luke records Paul's initial visit to Thessalonica during Paul's second missionary journey. So, when Paul, Timothy, and Silas arrived in Thessalonica, they spent three weeks teaching and preaching in the synagogues. Acts 17:2-3, NIV, records this and says:

'As was his custom, Paul went into the synagogue, and on three Sabbath days, he reasoned with them from the Scriptures, explaining and proving that the Messiah had to suffer and rise from the dead. "This Jesus I am proclaiming to you is the Messiah."'

And in response to Paul's preaching, there were some Jewish, many Greeks, and Paul persuaded some prominent women who accepted Christ as their Savior.

But, not all the people who were in the city appreciated Paul. Some became jealous and hired thugs from the marketplace to form a mob, and they started a riot in the city. The crowd stormed and broke into Paul and Silas's house.

And when they did not find Paul and Silas in the house, the mob drug the owner of the house, whose name was Jason, along with some other brothers in the home to face the city officials. By claiming Jesus is King, it was treason against Caesar. And while Jason and the other brothers were released on bail that night, Paul, Timothy, and Silas were smuggled out of town under cover of darkness. Yup, Paul and his friends socially distance themselves from the people of Thessalonica!

And they went from there to a place called Berea, which was about 50 miles from Thessalonica. When the mob learned they were in Berea, they saddled up their camels and headed to Berea and stirred up more trouble for Paul, which forced him to go to the coast, and take a ship to Athens to escape their violence. But Timothy and Silas stayed in Berea.

After some time had passed, Paul reunited with Timothy and Silas in Corinth. However, Paul was still concerned about the church in Thessalonica because it was a young church, and he had to leave in such a hurry. So, Paul sent Timothy to Thessalonica because he wanted to 'strengthen and encourage them in their faith.'

When Timothy returned with news from Thessalonica, Paul was in Corinth and wrote both of his letters to the church there and responded to Timothy's report of their faith and struggles.

As Paul writes in his letter today, the church at Thessalonica is remarkable. In that, when they came to know the Lord Jesus Christ as their Savior, it meant a total life change, and the result of their changed lives was that they caught the attention of a watching world. As Paul suggests that when a church gets on fire for the Lord, people will take notice, but it is not just people who take note, the Lord takes notice as well.

Which brings us back to the question, **"How can our faith reveal that God's mercy is still living among us today?"**

Our faith-filled witness frees us from holding on to hostile forces that seek to keep us in bondage because, as people of faith, we are to be liberated people, known with a new identity, an identity marked by goodness and mercy.

And we do our best to uphold this identity of being God's love and light in the world. Our presence in the national call for Mourning in Unity vigil last Monday, and again, with even more houses of faith participating, tomorrow evening, is, yes, another example of how we join with our neighbors in prayer for justice and peace on behalf of everyone, everywhere!

And we see that Moses also examples this kind of inclusive love for us today when he intercedes on behalf of the people of Israel and goes before God to ask that God continues with them on their journey to the promised land.

Sheila Harvey

And because Moses is humble and shares his need for God, God not only agrees to be with them on the journey, but God also reveals a glimpse of the divine glory to Moses.

God meets us on our level. God meets us right where we are and attempts to have a relationship with us. This exchange between God and Moses is a great model of how we are to be in a relationship with God and pray for one another.

And in seeing the examples of Moses and Paul, we see that our faith, love, and hope do not come without effort. That is why we must make a significant effort and spread the word about the importance of our vote in the upcoming elections. Because voting is an act of love, it shows that we believe in justice, peace, and freedom, for all people!

As we shared in our Bible Study last week, God calls upon our nation to live in an 'open society' for all of humanity instead of a 'closed society' that divides us, one from another. [90]

Today's message calls upon believers to decide whether our faith will be one of two things, either active or inactive. But when Paul writes in verse 3, "Remembering without ceasing your work of faith, a labor of love, and patience of hope in our Lord Jesus Christ, in the sight of God and our Father." [91]

Because when Paul preached these words, they received the Word of God and responded favorably to it. Even after Paul went away from their city, the church continued to thrive because the Gospel was its central message. As Paul says, 'we came preaching the Gospel of God's love, but not in the words of wisdom of men, in the power of the Holy Spirit.' [92]

Paul saw the manifestation of the Thessalonians' love in how they exerted themselves to do the work of Christ. Because of their sacrificial love, the Thessalonians were willing to labor for Christ gladly. Like so many of us, who have served in this church faithfully throughout the years.

And that is why, like the Thessalonian church and the people of Israel, we can be assured of God's eternal love for believers today because the love that has been given to us by God cannot and will not be removed.

And that is why we can sing with the psalmist who reminds us of God's sovereignty at work, through our justice and equity efforts, so that all might come to know God's perfect peace here on earth as it is in heaven!

So then, let us continue bringing our whole selves to God and being the living messages who give witness to God's goodness and mercy. Let us do so by allowing God to guide us from our bondage of negativity into our having the freedom to show love actively. And let our loving acts free us from the brokenness in our personal lives, towards each other, and with everyone, everywhere. May Jesus Christ continue to light the way. **AMEN.**

PRAYER

Almighty God, you promise us freedom and the opportunity to live in loving relationships with one another. May our love for you, O God, overflow into being a healing witness that cares for every neighbor, as exampled through Jesus Christ. **Amen.**

The Compassionate Life

How might God's vision of compassionate living give us hope?

Sunday, October 25, 2020
Twentieth Sunday after Pentecost

The Compassionate Life
This Sunday, we hear Jesus summarize the most significant law in two succinct commandments: love God and love your neighbor as you love yourself. Each of today's scripture passages promises that there is power in love which is at the heart of living a compassionate life.

So, let us ask, **"How might God's vision of compassionate living give us hope?"**

Jesus suggests that we first open our hearts to God's love so that we can, secondly, experience God's compassion working through us.

When the former first lady speaks to America and tells us to vote like our lives depend on it, it gets our attention. And when we read that there will be a Civil War on November 4, which is election day, we pause in shock. In looking at the world around us, we better understand how the early believers could have become emotionally, physically, and spiritually exhausted with the tension happening all around them.

But, to better understand what was happening during the time Jesus spoke with those early believers, it is essential to note that Jesus was talking with the religious leaders known as the Pharisees. They took the idea of knowing God and knowing God's word seriously. And this was the most incredible instruction in their lives.

That is why, when Jesus came into their presence, the Pharisees brought to Jesus a topic they had debated for years, which was whether they could determine the most important command of all the commandments.

So, many of us learn the ten commandments. Well, in rabbinical writings, it is understood that the law teachers had determined that there were 613 commandments in the Old Testament Law. [93] They classified 248 laws as positive commands, such as "do this…" or the "thou shalt." They organized the remaining 365 laws as negative commands such as "don't do this" or the "thou shalt not."

Pharisees were teachers of the law, and they classified each rule in the order of importance. But, Jesus' response to the Pharisees teaches us that even the most minor parts of the law are essential.

Jesus said that He had come to fulfill the Law, the whole Law. [94] Because Jesus understood that the question had to do with which command was the fundamental premise on which the rest of the law could be understood and practiced.

And that is why Jesus responds to their question from a section of the Old Testament called the Shema. It is found in Deut. 6 and is part of a passage recited by many Jewish believers at the start of every day and synagogue services. It says,

"Attention, Israel! God, our God! God the one and only! Love God, your God, with your whole heart: love him with all that's in you; love him with all you've got! Write these commandments that I've given you today in your hearts.

Get them inside of you, and then get them inside your children. Talk about them wherever you are, sitting at home or walking in the street; talk about them from the time you get up in the morning to when you fall into bed at night. Tie them on your hands and foreheads as a reminder; inscribe them on the doorposts of your homes and your city gates." (Deuteronomy 6:4-9, MSG)

Jesus used this Law to respond to the question of the religious leaders, which tells them that the command to love God with all your heart, soul, and mind is the first and most significant of all the commandments.

As Jesus emphasizes, this was a sacrificial kind of love. It is the kind of love that seeks to look out for the other person. It is not just a feeling, but it also requires a decision. And that is the kind of loving heart we seek for God.

As Ezekiel 36:26, NIV examples this love when the Lord says, "I will give you a new heart, and put a new spirit within you; I will take the heart of stone out of your flesh and give you a heart of flesh."

And, when we open our hearts for God, the kind of love that Jesus speaks of will infiltrate our hearts, souls, and minds; because Jesus wants us to understand that this love comes from the very depths of our being. It is what satisfies our deepest needs. It is what occupies our deepest thoughts and imaginations. It is an all-consuming kind of love that we experience when we open our hearts so that God can use it.

So, then, **"How might God's vision of compassionate living give us hope?"**

As we are taught by scriptures, by opening our hearts to receive God's love, we will learn how best to love ourselves and, in turn, become more loving towards one another.

Jesus teaches us we are to look out for others. [95] And that is why after giving the most significant law provided to the Pharisees, Jesus also shares the parable of the Samaritan, which is found in Luke 10, as Jesus broadens the definition of neighbor to mean anyone, we encounter with a need.

We open our hearts to loving God and neighbor. It is a vision that calls upon us to continuously seek and surrender to God, especially as God's love helps us in our daily living and guides us faithfully as a church.

And we see this kind of loving and faithful guidance in today's Old Testament scripture when God guides Moses and the people of Israel toward the land of promise. As we learn, they had wandered without a place to call home for 40 years before they would live into the promise of God. Moses offered this sacrificial love when he left being part of Pharaoh's home with every luxury imaginable to lead a people without a home.

And we also see this kind of love in the life of Jesus, as He leaves His heavenly home to come here on earth to offer the ultimate sacrifice and offered His body so that all of God's people can enter God's heavenly home!

As today's psalmist reminds us, God's promise of compassion is from everlasting to everlasting and that even in our disappointments, we are to find the joy that comes from trusting in the liberating vision of God for us to live out a compassionate life.

And we can almost hear Moses say, just as Martin Luther King, Jr. would later reveal, just before his assassination, that he had a vision of what the promised land might be like for humanity. Still, he also had a keen sense that he may not get there with us. [96] Because Moses, like Dr. King, had every reason to feel exhausted, discouraged, and heartbroken but, 'his sight was not impaired.' [97] In that, for Moses, the vision of the promised land was not limited to the physical territory the people were about to enter. The promised land also resided in freedom and justice for all people.

And this is something the Israelites and the author of Deuteronomy would soon forget as there is a story of genocide and brutal practices that would come from them towards the Canaanites, which was the same kind of treatment the Israelites had received in Egypt. And even here in America, whose founders sought freedom and crafted the liberating words, 'freedom and justice for all.' [98] But brutal treatment towards others would soon follow, and we struggle to live into these words, even today.

But, in Jesus Christ, we find hope. As it is clear, no matter who you are or where you come from, God is calling upon us all to be the beloved community by embracing the power of compassionate love. Because when we wholeheartedly see that all we have, comes from God's love, we will be able to live out God's vision of seeing each other, as sisters and brothers, who God equally loves. And we will be able to bless others in Godly love.

So, let us keep our sights on God's promise that we can have the kind of compassionate love here on earth, as it is in heaven. May it be so. **AMEN.**

PRAYER

God of all, help our words and deeds be a consistent witness to your love for everyone, everywhere. May we continually be shaped as a community where your passion is seen and known in all we are. **Amen.**

LETTER TWENTY-NINE

Partners in Service

How might we act as equal partners in Godly service?

<u>Sunday, November 1, 2020</u>
<u>Twenty-Second Sunday after Pentecost</u>

Partners in Service
On this day of Remembrance, the scripture readings call upon the early believers to remember to follow God, treat each other as equals, and become service partners for all the beloved community.

And so, **"How might we act as equal partners in Godly service?"**

As the scriptures suggest, if we <u>1) live according to what we believe, then 2) our acts of equitable love will be seen and known as serving all of God's beloved community.</u>

As Jesus is straightforward, God created us all as equal citizens when He tells His followers that titles and positions are not what matters most to God, but God is most concerned about our hearts. Jesus certainly speaks of equality amongst the believers because the religious leaders challenged His authority. This statement of equality for all saw growing tension between the synagogue and the followers of Jesus.

Sheila Harvey

But, Jesus reminds the believers that living out one's faith should be done in the community. In other words, Jesus does not want them to fall into the trap of anything that would undermine their ability to love the entire beloved community that God so loves. And that is why Jesus says that to be a leader, one must be willing to work with others by being a servant leader. [99]

And then, after the resurrection of Jesus, Paul comes along and offers us an excellent example of what Jesus meant by Godly love as Paul writes a letter to the church in Thessalonica, which is in modern-day Greece. In that, his letter encourages and lifts the members of this early church by telling them that they are a community rooted in God's grace and love. Paul hopes that they will continue serving God despite their challenges by faithfully serving others. And so, Paul tells them that, regardless of the challenges that come their way, they are a family of faith committed to Jesus Christ. Paul reminds them they have seen the Holy Spirit at work.

And that is why, Paul writes in 1 Thessalonians 2:9, ESV, "For you remember, sisters and brothers, our labor and toil; night and day." As Paul reminded those early believers, when he worked among them, they needed to continue working and toiling together as faithful partners, in service, together.

Paul shares the importance of living what they believe, even in the face of their challenges as a church. And it is for these reasons of servant leadership exampled Paul continues to see a lot of good in the early church.

Like Jesus and Paul, who spoke about the importance of being partners in faithful service to God, many years ago, the bishops in England thought there were many good people to offer in remembrance. So much so that they declared, there should be one day, set apart, to commemorate all who had lived Godly lives. And so, November 1 was then designated as "All Saints Day."

But, we also see that when Paul wrote his letter to the Christians living in Rome, the address he put on the envelope was, "To all in Rome, who are loved of God, and called to be saints." (Romans 1:7, KJV). And like all of

170

us, they were not perfect. But also, like each of us, they were precious, in God's sight.

Another excellent example of God's equal love for us all is in the story of a young boy sent to the corner store by his mother to buy a loaf of bread. The boy was gone much longer than it should have taken him. And so, when he finally returned, his mother asked, *"Where have you been? I have been worried sick about you."* "Well," he answered, "there was a little boy with a broken bike who was crying. So, I stopped to help him." *"I did not know, you knew anything, about fixing bikes," his mother said.* "I do not," he replied. "I just stayed there and cried with him." [100] What a great way to be a partner in Christ's service!

And so, **"How might we act as equal partners in Godly service?"**

We have been holding each other as equal partners of the beloved community through our prayers during the Monday night candlelight vigils. As scriptures suggest, "Every Member is a Minister," or "Every believer, is a Minister, and a servant of Christ," which means that as members of the Body of Christ, we are all ministers partnering in Christ's service.

This partnering means that everyone is welcome to offer their whole selves to the church, just as the sharing of gifts was encouraged in the early church. God has given us all gifts to share, and each contribution is essential to Christ's church. Nothing is too small or too big. And as Paul puts it, we all can contribute to doing God's work.

But, like the early church, we might need some inspiration and encouragement along the way. And that is what we hear in our reading of Joshua today, as Joshua's leadership speaks of the shared responsibility necessary to ensure that everyone crosses the waters safely. This story is another example of God's call for us to care for everyone boldly.

A classic example of what happens when we are not bold in our faith is a famous, old fable passed down for generations. It tells of an older man traveling with a boy and a donkey. And, as they walked through a village, the man was leading the donkey, and the boy was walking behind. The townspeople said the older man was a fool for not riding, so to please them; he climbed up on the animal's back. When they came to the next village, the people said the older man was cruel to let the child walk while enjoying the ride. So, to please them, he got off, set the boy on the animal's back, and continued his way. In the third village, people accused the child of being lazy for making the older man walk, and they suggested that both should ride. So, the man climbed on, and they set off again. In the fourth village, the townspeople were indignant at the cruelty to the donkey because he carried two people. And the frustrated man was last seen, carrying the donkey down the road.

This story reminds us of what can happen when we are not bold and try to please others instead of pleasing God. Because, even with challenges, our faith instructs us to seek God's guidance in our personal lives and for the greater community.

So, when we think about our community, its history, where it began, and where it is today, we see that it could only have been made possible with God leading the way. Members have been partners in service through the years. Union is a church of many firsts here in West Palm Beach. Union's servant leaders started the first hospital, started the first library, and started the first schoolhouse.

As a welcoming church, Union also embraces God's equitable love for everyone, which is evident in calling its first full-time woman, and African-American to serve as its pastor. We lost a couple of members over that vote. But, Union's welcome for all people did not stop there as Union made it clear that it is okay for its pastor to marry gays and lesbians. We lost quite a few more members over that vote. However, Union ultimately realized that to fully embrace the teachings of Jesus Christ, who teaches us that we are to love everyone equally, we unanimously voted to become a church that seeks justice and peace for everyone, everywhere.

Being called partners in Christ's service forces us to choose what kind of Christians we will be, either following God's teachings or going along with what others say we should do. Being called as partners in Christ's service challenges us to be bold in our efforts to seek God's equitable love, even if it is unpopular for us to do so. Being partners in Christ's service makes us take a good look at ourselves, to see whether we care about justice for some or whether we care about justice for all. And being partners in Christ's service holds each other accountable for getting out to VOTE in civic elections as Union has been a voting site in the community for many, many years.

And so, let the stories tell of our past, inform our present, and inspire our future as we, prayerfully, move forward, together, as partners, in a ministry of Godly service. May it be so. **AMEN.**

PRAYER

Almighty God, you hold all the powers of the universe within your hands. We give thanks for the loving ways you light our path and keep us in the ways of hope. Guide us in your caring ways. Amen.

Tending God's Light

How can we keep our light shining for God?

<u>Sunday, November 8, 2020</u>
<u>Twenty-Third Sunday after Pentecost</u>

Tending God's Light
On this Veterans Sunday, we hear stories in the scriptures that teach believers to remain faithful in their relationship with God. The Gospel of Matthew passage examples for us the importance of the bridesmaids **tending their lights** to be ready to shine their lights when the bridegroom, Jesus Christ, comes.

And so, as we reflect upon this ancient story, our question for today could be, **"How can we keep our light shining for God?"**

Today's readings suggest that we <u>first keep God's light burning within us so that we can secondly be ready to live as loving witnesses of God's love by our light.</u>

It is important to note that the story about the bridesmaids is a beautiful example of how the church is very special to Jesus. Because Jesus died to bring the church into existence and His love for the church is what gives us hope. The church is called the Bride of Jesus Christ, and Christ is the Bridegroom.

Sheila Harvey

This story allows us to look at a typical Jewish wedding. The scene of this parable focuses on ten Bridesmaids who prepare for a wedding banquet that is to take place in the home of the groom. [101]

And in great anticipation, there is a large crowd of family and friends filling the groom's home, and they pour out into the street in front of the dwelling. And as the group gathers, the groom and several close friends are making their way to the bride's home, which is assumed to be across town or in a nearby village.

From there, the groom greets his bride and escorts her back to his family home, where the crowd awaits, and the marriage feast will occur. When the bride was ready, she would go on the back of a riding animal, and the groom, with his friends, would form an exuberant parade.

This happy group would then take the longest possible route back to the groom's home so that most of the people could see and cheer them as they passed. Some of the crowd would wait in the street at the groom's house as they anticipated the wedding party's arrival.

But, another aspect of this story is that it takes place at night. And among the guests are ten young women. Each of them has a lamp, and of course, all ten lamps are in use. Half of them have brought extra oil in a small flask, while the other half had not taken this precaution.

And so, as the parade was winding slowly through the village, it took a bit longer than they anticipated. And as the young women became drowsy, they carefully placed their burning lamps on a window ledge and dozed off outside the house.

So, when the front of the parade finally enters the alley leading to the groom's house, the cry goes out, "Behold the bridegroom. Come out to meet him." [102] The guests and the family still in the house rush into the street. And the ten young women are awakened and begin to "service their lamps" by adjusting the wicks to ensure the oil reserves inside the lamps.

Then, we learn that five of the women suddenly realize their lamps are almost out of olive oil and have no reserves. The other five take out their little clay flasks and calmly replenish their lamps. Then, the groom and his new bride arrive, and the entire crowd sweeps into the house and shuts the door.

The five women finally acquire some oil, get their lamps working again, and arrive home in the final scene. And they shout through the door, "Lord! Open to us!" But, the groom's reply is, "I do not know you." [103]

Jesus teaches this story to encourage believers to remain patient when we hope for something taking longer than expected to happen. Jesus encourages the believers to hold on to their faith by tending to it and nurturing it. So, when it is time to do the work that God calls upon us to do, believers will be known by the light they shine for God and towards one another.

Therefore, when we ask the question, **"How can we keep our light shining for God?"**

We can respond by shining our God-given light daily so that we offer ourselves peace during the ever-present conflict, hope amid life's continuous uncertainties, and love, that acts to serve God, and everyone, everywhere.

And on this Sunday, as we honor our nation's veterans, it is fitting to share the story of Ron Coker of Nebraska, who received his draft notice and enlisted in the Marine Corps shortly after high school graduation. For his bravery in saving a fellow marine, he was later honored for his service.

In that, this vigilant service turns us to the story of Joshua. As he tells the people of Israel to 'Choose this day, whom you will serve.' [104] And he calls upon the people to act in faith and trust in God, who can bring good out of evil.

And that is why we are here today. We are here because we trust in God. We trust that God will help us stay awake or, as the young folks say, help us to stay woke and be ready to serve. We are here to worship, despite the evil that exists in our world, because, like the psalmist says, 'we are to tell of God's might and the wonders that God has done.' [105]

We are here because we believe that Christ's light shines for the unity of humanity so that healing and peace will be possible for everyone, everywhere. We are here because we believe that love wins when we shine Christ's light in our lives for the sake of others. And we are here as witnesses to those believers past and present, who live their lives tending God's light, of freedom, liberty, and justice for all. May God continue to lead the way forward. **Amen.**

PRAYER

God in your mercy, help us do all we can to trust in your generosity, presence, and goodness. Guide us as a community of faith to invest ourselves spiritually, emotionally, and physically in sharing God's love with the world. Amen.

LETTER THIRTY-ONE

Extravagant Opportunity

How might we boldly use our gifts and talents to please God?

Sunday, November 15, 2020
Twenty-Fourth Sunday after Pentecost

Extravagant Opportunity
Today, we hear stories about God's extravagant opportunity for people of faith. These early believers are encouraged to use their gifts and talents by rejecting their fears of scarcity instead of trusting in God's abundant love.

And in hearing this, let us ask, **"How might we boldly use our gifts and talents to please God?"**

These passages teach us 1) to recognize that God has blessed us with every good thing we have so that 2) we can selflessly serve God by being a blessing to others.

And this message of God's faithful giving is at the core of the story we hear in today's reading, found in Joshua when we learn that God is displeased because the believers did not appreciate the blessings of God. And for their lack of faithfulness, they were put under the control of foreigners.

But, even during their turning away from God, God's faithfulness shows up, and they receive an extravagant opportunity to change their ways and to live for God.

God offers them grace by sending a judge named Deborah, who happens to be the only female judge of her time, as she leads the effort to deliver them from their foreign oppression. God uses Deborah, who acts as a judge and acts as a prophet because she hears and speaks for God. In that, Deborah is an example of someone who puts her God-given gifts to work, and her skills and talents were multiplied in surprising, creative, and inspiring ways on behalf of those early believers.

We also see that using gifts and talents is highlighted in today's gospel lesson as the parable of the talents in Matthew warns against burying a blessing that God has given.

Jesus tells us that the master represents God, and the servants represent us because we learn that each person was given money which is also known as talents, and they were given these talents based upon their ability to make the most of it. As the servant with five talents began to invest and work his master's money, he doubled the money when it was all said and done. So, when the master settled accounts with him, the servant returned ten talents. And it was the same with the servant given two talents doubling the master's money and returning four skills to the master.

However, we learn that the third servant who had only one talent did not bother to use it or even invest it. He just dug a hole in the ground and buried it.
And that is why the master said, "You could have at least put it in the bank, so it could have gained interest." [106]

Making the most of what we have is found in the 'dash' of our lives from birth until earthly death. The 'dash' is often mentioned during 'celebration of life services,' when people have lived a life filled with many blessings. And an example that we all should use the opportunities given to us by sharing them with others in the 'dash' of our lives.

Jesus teaches about the blessing of talents when He says that the master did not give these talents to be stored in a place for safekeeping. But instead, the master's intent was for the servants to invest the skills they had been given, which meant that they had to take a risk. They had to overcome a fear of scarcity that there would not be enough and trust in the abundance of God.

Let us now go back to our question, **"How might we boldly use our gifts and talents to please God?"**

As we can refer to Matthew 25:29, NKJV, which says, "For to all those who have, more will be given, and they will have an abundance. But from those who have nothing, even what they have will be taken away."

This scripture was probably in the mind of the one who crafted the old saying, "Nothing ventured, nothing gained." Or the other popular motto says, "If you do not succeed the first time, try, try, again." As we all know that success is not always automatic because it usually takes time and effort for an investment to become profitable.

There also are several examples in the history books, full of stories, about gifted persons whose talents were overlooked until someone believed in them.

A few examples of talented people who remained faithful and invested in their gifts include:

Einstein, who was four years old before he could speak, and seven, before he could read, became one of the greatest physicists who ever lived. [107]

Another person using their gifts is Fannie Lou Hamer, who tirelessly persevered, to cast her vote. And as the story goes, the day after learning at a church service of her legal right to vote, she went to cast her vote but was run out of town, jailed, and beaten nearly to death for trying to exercise her right to vote. She shared her knowledge of the scriptures and sang hymns to spread God's love for humanity in those moments. And because of her faithfulness to God, she did not quit in her struggle for justice. As Mrs.

Hamer not only would later cast her vote in Mississippi, but she also would become a significant figure at the Democratic Convention of 1964. [108]

And the last person is one of the most famous names in the world, Walt Disney, who was "fired by a newspaper… because he reportedly had "no good ideas." [109] And it is also written that Disney started in Kansas City in his early years and could not even sell his cartoons. Some even hinted that he had no talent. But Disney had a dream, so he set out to conquer his foes. He found a minister who paid him a small amount to draw advertising pictures for his church. And since Disney had no place to stay, the church let him sleep in the mouse-infested garage. And guess what, one of those mice, Disney nicknamed Mickey, whose name has become famous worldwide.

As it is clear, each of these people had one thing in common: their willingness to take the risk of investing in themselves and applying their God-given gifts and talents that became a great blessing to others.

This church is a beautiful example of people investing their talents by serving others, and that is just what Jesus teaches us, a good servant should be. We work together to create extravagant welcoming opportunities for all of God's people throughout the years. We continue supporting homeless families in our area throughout the year by helping to feed the community throughout the year and by partnering with our neighbors to help create a more just society for the sake of peace and amongst all God's children in the world.

And we also offer extravagant opportunities towards one another as the Body of Christ by visiting, calling, and praying with those who are sick. We not only serve our community and church family, we first and foremost, serve and worship God by offering ourselves as virtual live-streaming worshippers, by being COVID-19 mask wearers, by serving as Sunday School and Bible virtual Zoomers, being Union's ministry leaders, peaceful justice advocates and so much more.

And that is why we, as a beloved community of faith, continue to be so very blessed because the presence of God is in our midst, reminding us just how fortunate we are. We are blessed with an extravagant opportunity to be the church of Jesus Christ, a church that means it when we say, 'No matter who you are, or where you are from, you are welcome here!'

And so, let us trust that God has given us gifts and talents for them to multiply beyond what we know to ask for or even imagine! Let us also, faithfully, rely on God's justice, like today's psalmist who says, 'I look my eyes up, to the sovereign, O God, until God has mercy on us.' [110] And, let us not give up hope, as we **move forward, to see, what the end will bring** believing, that God's love can multiply inside of our hearts within the church and outward, into the world guiding us to reject fears of scarcity, and to receive, instead, God's abundant joy. May it be so, now and always. **AMEN.**

PRAYER

Generous God, provider of manna in the wilderness, and daily bread from heaven, we thank you for your Holy Word. As we worship and give thanks, inspire us to hunger for bread that is life-giving. **Amen.**

Reigning Compassion

What challenges prevent us from responding in love to the most vulnerable?

<u>Sunday, November 22, 2020</u>
<u>Reign of Christ Sunday/ Thanksgiving Sunday</u>

Reigning Compassion
This Thanksgiving Sunday, we celebrate the Reign of Christ, also known as Christ the King, Sunday. Jesus Christ offers an open invitation to those early Christians to follow in the way of His reigning compassion to the most vulnerable by calling upon them to love and live, with justice and peace, here on earth.

So, let us ask, **"What challenges prevent us, from both seeing and responding in love, to the most vulnerable among us?"**

The scripture suggests that we <u>1) see Christ's presence among those often ignored so that we 2) respond with dignity and respect by caring for every neighbor equally.</u>

Those around the church for a while know that one of our favorite hymns is "God's Eye Is on the Sparrow." Because it answers the question that we have during those moments of uncertainty, and grief which is "God, do you see me?" Jesus is speaking directly to this question to the early believers when He brings to light the people who are suffering. [111]

Jesus goes on to make clear how believers are to understand and live in the faithfulness to the commandments that all the laws and prophets hang, and says, 'You shall love the Lord your God..." and "You shall love your neighbor as you love yourself." [112]

Then, Jesus poses the question of whether they see Him. He speaks about the hungry thirsty, those who we call the stranger, those who are naked, sick, and imprisoned. Because, according to Jesus, if love allows us to see those who suffer who are the least among us, we also see Christ.

Biblical scholars refer to this week's Gospel message as the "Last Judgment" because of the 'end times of Jesus's coming. But, if we look closer, we see that this message of love does not have to do with those who believe the 'right' thing about Jesus or those who belong to the 'right' religious tradition. The final judgment has to do with a theological metaphor that directly addresses the commandment of our loving God and our loving neighbor. This apocalyptic coming of Jesus' story has to do with whether we will choose to see the most vulnerable and respond with God's reigning compassion and love.

Now, with these words in our hearts, let us return to our question, **"What challenges prevent us, from both seeing and responding in love, to the most vulnerable among us?"**

We can naturally feel overwhelmed by the challenges of caring for the stranger, clothing the naked, giving water to the thirsty, feeding the hungry, and visiting the imprisoned. Still, we can also take comfort in knowing that we are all equally loved by God and will of ourselves, joyfully especially, to those who have the most need.

And that is why the story of Ezekiel imagines an end time, in which a clear distinction is made, between living in faithfulness to God's liberation and justice or aligning one's life with the forces of oppression. Psalm 100 is also a vital and essential reminder that having a genuine love of God, and having a life of deep joy, go hand in hand. Seeing with one's heart helps us see with hope, and the working of Jesus Christ, where the fullness of God's compassionate love, peace, and justice resides.

Overcoming challenges is told in a story about a dad with six kids, stressed over money for shoes, who meets a couple with one son unable to wear shoes. At that moment, his blessings came into view.

But perhaps, some of us are not feeling blessed during this season. Maybe it is too difficult to see the gifts that God has given. Maybe the pain of life has been so overwhelming that there is no way to see many blessings. Or perhaps even those blessings we recognized before do not look all that good anymore.

For those who feel that way, the prayer is that we can begin to focus more on what we have, rather than simply focusing on what we do not have, to see if it changes our view because it is hard to see and respond as blessings to others if we cannot see the gifts of God in our own lives.

So, when we seek to love and live in the way of Jesus Christ, here are some things to consider:

1) To be thankful that we do not already have everything we want so we can look forward to what is to come.
2) Be thankful when we do not know something; this allows us to learn.
3) Be thankful for the difficult times because, during those times, we can grow.
4) Be thankful for each new challenge because it can build our strength and character.
5) Be thankful for our mistakes. They can teach us valuable lessons. And last,
6) Be thankful when we are tired and weary. Because it means that we have made a difference.

Our gratitude will help us see God's love in us and others. Because we never know who God might use to offer us blessings in our times of need.

Sheila Harvey

There is a gratitude story, perfect, for this time of year, about a woman, who was visiting some people who lived on a farm, and she noticed a pig limping in the backyard with a wooden leg. [113] So, she asked the farmer, "What happened to the pig?" The farmer said, "Oh, Betsy is a wonderful pig."

One night the house caught fire, and she oinked so loud she woke us, and we got the fire truck in time to save the place." The woman said, "That's something!" The farmer continued, "That is not all, one day, my youngest fell in the pond, and Betsy oinked so loud that she got our attention, and we were able to pull my daughter out of the pond in time." The woman said, "That is amazing!"

But, I still do not understand why the pig has a wooden leg. Then, the farmer said, "Well, when you have a pig that special, you do not want to eat him all at once!" Gratitude only went so far for the three-legged hero.

But, here at Union, our gratitude runs deep! Especially as we celebrate 126 years of being God's church here in West Palm Beach. And as we continue to believe that God has more light to bring forth in this place and more bread from heaven, for us to share with our neighbors near and far.

And so, let us offer our sincere gratitude of thanks for 'The Bread of Life,' which is Jesus Christ. Let us give thanks for the opportunity to faithfully 'show up' to worship, even virtually!! Let us give thanks to our deacons and others who continue to reach out to our family of faith!! Thanks to our volunteers who continue to serve others through our caring, justice, and peace ministries. And let us accept the invitation of Jesus Christ to offer compassion in the world by faithfully loving God, loving ourselves, and loving others as we love ourselves. May it be so. **Amen.**

CHAPTER THREE

THE SEASON OF ADVENT

Letters for the Season of Advent come amid the rise of national political tensions, the looming global pandemics of COVID-19, and systemic racial injustice, along with the first round of vaccines for older adults.

PRAYER

Loving God, as you guide us, offer us hopeful possibilities for all humanity so that we might see in the Christ story ourselves. AMEN.

LETTER THIRTY-THREE

Where are You, God?

How do we wait with hope for something greater to come?

<u>Sunday, November 29, 2020</u>
<u>First Sunday of Advent</u>

Where Are You, God?
On this First Sunday of Advent, the early believers ask, 'Where are you, God,' as they wait in anticipation for Christ's love to come into the world.

And so, like the early believers, we also ask, **"How do we wait with anticipation, the hope of something greater to come?"**

As the scriptures teach us that <u>if we are to 1) remain in hopeful anticipation of God's faithfulness, then we will 2) become witnesses to the everlasting presence of God.</u>

This year, with the coronavirus wiping out more than a quarter-of-a-million Americans in such a short time frame, we have been forced to pause from our' business as usual' lifestyle and, in effect, become still so that we can reflect upon what Christ's coming, truly means. The material things that are usually at the top of our Christmas lists are now replaced, by our hopes and wishes, for good health, family time, zoom gatherings, and the rallying cry for equal treatment, towards all people.

And in today's gospel lesson, we are invited to change our 'business as usual' attitude that cares for the interests of a few and takes on the 'business of Christ's love' attitude that cares for all people. This new season of Advent calls upon us to reshape, reclaim, and remember why we are to put Christ's loving care at the top of every Christmas list, not only this year but on any given year.

Mark's gospel beautifully illustrates the power of our Creating God, who created the sun, the moon, and the sky. By offering us a lesson from the fig tree, to remind us that every newly created season of life presents another opportunity to prepare ourselves for what is to come. Like this story, every believer is to do the same by taking on the business of being God's love in the world.

Now, let us return to our question, **"How do we wait with anticipation, the hope of something greater to come?"**

In a nation divided, it is essential to remember that as we wait for Jesus Christ, to reveal the love that we anticipate, we can consider the decisions we make and how we treat others as we look to participate in the reconciling love of God.

Like the early church going through a difficult time of societal unrest, we are also experiencing societal concerns around the issues of justice and peace. It leaves us wanting real hope for equal justice and genuine peace amongst all of us, God's creation.

God's presence in the world offers us the possibility, the hope, and the assurance of God revealed in our lives and the world.

In that, today's reading from the prophet Isaiah helps us to understand the anticipation and preparation of life better, especially as we enter the season of Advent. On one side of this Advent journey, it takes us on the path to Bethlehem with a star shining down on the manger.

And on the other side of this journey, it takes us on the path that reminds us that ultimately God will come, but when, where, or how we do not know. And yet, we see this kind of hopeful fulfillment is possible when the prophet Isaiah writes to those who have returned from exile, only to discover that restoring a nation and a community. Restoring faith is long, challenging, and even depressing work. So, they began to look for the One who would bring hope into their despair because they longed for God's presence in their emptiness and a way of being in a world they no longer recognized.

One group holds on to what has always been, and those exiled bring a different perspective on who they are as people of God. Both groups remember. Both groups were trying to proclaim what they lost during the exile. Both groups were trying to reshape who they are as the people of God together.

And in these moments, the prophet, Isaiah, cries out with one voice, for both groups, who look for God to break open the heavens as Isaiah laments and calls for the people of God to confess brokenness and reclaim the ways that God is reshaping and molding all to become.

And as people of faith living in a divided nation, we can surely relate to the cries of Isaiah in wanting restoration.

Today's psalm is an outright plea for restoration as people in turmoil cling to the hope that comes from the promise of God. The hope that the one to come will restore the people and bring about wholeness and healing. This hope is evident in the recurring refrain, which says, 'Restore us, O Lord God of hosts; let your face shine, that we may be saved.' [114]

As the psalmist question, 'where are you, God,' is a desperate plea for God to show up but then, the psalmist ends with the realization that God has always been there.

And that is why we can join with the psalmist in singing praises to God who is with us, still! Hope brings about spiritual growth, which looks beyond what worries us and offers us the assurance that God is with us from everlasting to everlasting.

And so, as we enter this new Advent Season of waiting and preparing, let us remember that we are not waiting alone. This waiting time dismantles the current constructs that have shifted our focus from 'looking out for myself' into the attitude of 'being Christ's love for everyone,' [115] in the world.

This shift in focus gives us hope for those things, not as they are but as we hope they will someday become. In that, our world could use a little opening up and transforming. Because if change begins with us, then how we pray is a good place to start. Prayer is at work when it changes us. And advent is the season to expect God's presence and look for to the birth of something new and long-awaited. Perhaps we could pray for our transformations. Pray that our hearts open to more compassion. Let that desire for more love and understanding fill our hearts of a world longing for release from fear and prejudice, a world where people of faith long for a clear path to the heart of justice for all people and love shines for everyone, everywhere.

As we offer these prayers, let us bring our tears, all our laughter, and all our anxieties to God. Let us bring all our hopes and wishes for Christ's loving care in the world to the top of every Christmas list this and every season. Let us also consider the decisions we make and how we treat others as we carry on 'the business of offering loving care' towards all the beloved creation, now and even, until the very end. And let us allow Christ's light to guide us every step of the way. May it be so. **Amen.**

PRAYER

All-knowing God, awaken us to your coming and help us to mold all our worries into your peace. Amen.

LETTER THIRTY-FOUR

A Hope for Peace

How can our actions reinforce Christ's perfect peace?

<u>Sunday, December 6, 2020</u>
<u>Second Sunday of Advent</u>

A Hope for Peace
On this second Sunday in Advent, our scripture readings for today offer us hope for peace. The message to the early believers is that God's abiding presence lives within and among all of humanity.

And as believers today, let us ask, **"How can our actions reinforce Christ's perfect peace?"**

We can explore this question by first <u>reminding ourselves to replace our worries with the hope that God will provide a way through troubled times.</u>

And today, we hear the voice of God through the prophet Isaiah who says, "Prepare the way of the Lord!" [116] The people of Israel were in exile, in an unfamiliar place, and trying to understand their new reality.

The prophet reminds them to hold fast to who they are as God's people and make use of their time in exile to prepare. And verse three emphasizes the importance of working and organizing in their wilderness location.

The prophet refers to human beings like grass and flowers that wither and fade, yet God's Word remains.

As the final Word of the prophet speaks to God's provision, which means that God protects, provides, and cares for all of humanity even if it is different from what we expect. In that, God's provision gives comfort to the people of Israel even in the wilderness, as they prepare the way of God.

This message reflects the importance of God's love for migrants. And during this time of year, we would usually host our Annual Migrant Farmworkers Christmas Breakfast. Our Women's Fellowship ministry would welcome and unite with other women from local churches throughout the local area. And we would share the importance of our living out the hope that someday, all people would be treated with dignity. Then, we would close by singing Christmas carols reminding us of God's love with Ilsa banging away on the piano.

But, our time would not end after breakfast, nor would it end after singing the carols. Instead, we would all move into the Fellowship Hall, where clothes and toys that all the churches donated would fill the large Hall. And we would assist the coordinators of the Migrant Farmworker program in loading up the gifts, as they would transport all the contributions to the children of the migrant farmworkers.

And while we could not have our annual breakfast this year, the church decided to collect clothing and toys for the farmworker children. We are making this special effort because these children are not only the children of the farmworkers who pick our tomatoes and other crops in the Florida heat for a small amount of money. They are also the children of God as these migrant farmworkers make it possible for us to have fresh food in our restaurants and on our kitchen tables.

Now, let us return to our question, **"How can our actions reinforce Christ's peace?"**

We can begin with trusting in God's promise to show up and provide for all our needs. And by our trusting in God's faithfulness, we can also find the courage to act as messengers of hope by reflecting God's voice of justice and peace, which comforts all people.

This message of hopeful peace is what we hear today from our reading in Isaiah when we hear God saying, 'Comfort, comfort, O my people.' [117] As God is with us. In that, God wants us to know that no circumstance can separate us from God's love. And because of this, we are to be comforted, and we are to find peace in knowing that God loves us. And therefore, we are to remain hopeful in knowing that God cares.

And it was this comforting peace that was present among the migrant farmworkers who met with clergy and shared their stories about how they hoped for a better life. They spoke about how churches like ours helped bless workers by helping with clothes, food, and helping their human dignity.

As the migrant farmworkers and the migrants in Isaiah both, example God's promise of something great even amid the 'not-so-great' moments of life.

And that is why the psalmist today calls upon God's steadfast love because there are times in our lives when we need to feel the presence of God. Like the psalmist, we need to remember how far God has brought us in our lives because we alone could not get to this place without God's presence. And so, we join with the psalmist in asking to hear God speak peace into our lives so that we can feel God's eternal presence in our hearts.

Our faith gives us hope for the peace promised to each of us. And that kind of hopeful peace is what our Gospel message today in Mark's Gospel is all about. In that, it teaches us about John the Baptizer, whose job it was to tell people to remain hopeful in God, and he did so by telling them about the coming of Jesus Christ who would change them from the inside out and comfort them, even during their loss.

And God's voice is speaking to us, still. One of the best examples of peace beyond our understanding of significant loss is in the old hymn written by Horatio Spafford, "It is Well with My Soul." [118] The hymn is sparked by a tragic incident when his wife and four daughters' cruise ship was compromised, and the ship sank into the Atlantic Ocean.

After some time, only Horatio's wife, Anna, was rescued alive. After receiving notice of the wreckage, Horatio booked himself on the next available ship to join Anna. Upon his arrival, he wrote:

When peace like a river attendeth my way,
When sorrows like sea billows roll,
Whatever my lot, Thou hast taught me to say,
It is well; it is well with my soul.

So, let us embrace these heartfelt words and trust that this kind of peace surpasses all understanding. Let us trust that this kind of peace comes from expecting God to show up. And let us trust that when we prepare the way of the Lord, our daily acts of love will reflect Christ's love coming into the world for all of humanity. May it be so. **Amen.**

PRAYER

Faithful God, give us faith to live joyfully as we seek your way of hope, peace, and love. Help us focus on your mighty works by taking everything to you in prayer. And through your Spirit, help us find direction and purpose in all that each day brings. **Amen.**

LETTER THIRTY-FIVE

Shouts of Joy

How might we find joy, even during times of pain?

<u>Sunday, December 13, 2020</u>
<u>Third Sunday of Advent</u>

Shouts of Joy
On this third Sunday in Advent, the scripture invites the church to remain hopeful for the future by transforming our mourning into 'shouts of joy.'

And as we reflect upon this message, we may ask, **"How might we find joy, even during times of pain?"**

First, we can be joyful when we <u>first allow God into our hearts so that we can secondly be grateful for all the good that God has done.</u>

And in speaking to God's desire to comfort and provide for us, we hear the prophet Isaiah saying that out of our brokenness can come restoration and rejoicing. Today's reading of Isaiah begins with an introduction stating that God has sent him to declare a holy word of restoration for the people. The servant's words have power because they do not imply the importance of the servant but instead speak of the work of God restoring all things. The anointed messenger continues by stating that God will work through the people.

Sheila Harvey

The news of restoration that Isaiah brings is for the oppressed, broken-hearted, captives, and prisoners as each of these areas impacts the people of this time. The people had to leave their land, and they were in pain. The verse address both the pain of the people and speaks about the restorative nature of God. And that is why it is written; restoration and rejoicing can come out of our brokenness!

Today's psalmist reminds us how we might get to the point of rejoicing, even when believers are in pain. The psalmist also remarks on the good things that God had done and refers to the sheer joy that came when the people that Isaiah spoke of were no longer in exile. And yet, when the people returned to their homes, they had to build back what they lost. The psalmist thanks God for the past blessings, trusting God will continue to provide for the people's needs. And out of gratefulness for God's provision, the psalmist offers shouts of joy!

Now, let us return to our question, **"How might we find joy, even during times of pain?"**

Well, scripture teaches us that whatever our circumstances, we are to find the goodness of God and be grateful for what God has done, be thankful for what God is doing, and be thankful for what God will do. And that is why, in 1 Thessalonians, we hear the words, 'rejoice always.' It teaches us that in everything we do, we should rejoice in God, and in that rejoicing, we will be on our way to being healed from our pain.

But, we should not ignore pain. It is real. And it can impact us profoundly. Therefore, like physical pain, we should address emotional and spiritual pain to begin the healing process. And one way to manage the pain that festers, and can impact others, is by watching the Christmas Classic for kids The Grinch Who Stole Christmas! [119]

And in recent years, Union's kids and teens went to see this popular family movie because it is an excellent example of sharing our Christian message of why it is important to 'rejoice in the Lord always!'

208

This story, written by Dr. Seuss, tells of a disgruntled person named Grinch. And this grumpy character has no room in his heart for Christmas.

Every year, he worked himself into a rage because the Who's, the little people who lived in a place called Whoville, celebrated Christmas with a passion. They decorated their homes and their town. They celebrated with several feasts. They exchanged gifts and sang songs – but this bothered the Grinch. And so, the Grinch devised a plan.

As he thought to himself that if he could steal the decorations, steal the gifts, and steal the food from the feasts, then he could steal Christmas. Because the Who's would have nothing to celebrate, and so, Grinch executes his evil plan. He cleans out the village so that there is not enough feast left to feed a mouse.

As Christmas Day arrives, the Grinch is resting on a rugged cliff. Ready to throw all the Christmas items that he's stolen from the Who's over the edge. Then, he pauses for just a second hoping to hear wailing and whimpering from the Whoville village below. But instead, the Who's gather and sing just like they always had.

And when the Grinch hears the Who's singing, he finally realizes that Christmas is not about the gifts and the feasts and the decorations, but that there is something more significant and more considerable, something that the grouchiness of this world cannot stop. It is something that they look forward to with joy more extraordinary than the 'things' they will get that will make them happy at that moment and instead look forward with joy and praise with what they will receive from God that is eternal.

The psalmist refers to this kind of joy when singing; may those who sow in tears reap with shouts of joy. [120] In that, this is the kind of joy that looks beyond our temporary circumstances and trusts that God is still near. But, this kind of living requires faith. Believing and trusting so much so that no matter what happens through prayer, God will hear our needs, and the peace of God will enter our hearts—keeping us calm and enabling us to long for God's love, justice, and peace in every season of our lives.

Every week exercise this faith in worship as we offer our prayers and songs to God. We offer thanksgiving for our blessings. We are like the Who's in the town of Whoville and like John exampled in our reading today. We example how to 'be the voice shouting out in the wilderness,' [121] pointing out the way to the Life-light into the world because we are to believe in our hearts that there is not a situation nor a place that God cannot heal, nor redeem!

We see that God defeats death and shows the world the redemption of all creation through the life, death, and resurrection of Jesus Christ, and that is why we can believe in our hearts that God is guiding our lives so that we can return go out into the world as carriers of Christ's marvelous light.

As John's message, today asks, we make a joyful noise unto the Lord and allow God to bring joy and peace into our lives. And we are asked to make a joyful noise and allow God to bring us comfort through the Christ Child. We accept the invitation to make a joyful noise so that our Advent preparation will enable us to express the joy of salvation in our hearts in our faithful worship and the ways we seek to help make our world better.

Making our world better is something that we can do. And opening our hearts to God, and allowing God to use us, was what John the baptizer emphasized when he stated that we are to share our God-given lights. As John shared, we can all testify that we are not shining as the Light, but we can all attest to that light.

And so, let us be grateful for the light of Christ that brings good news to the poor. Let us be thankful that the light of Christ can heal the broken-hearted. Let us be grateful that the light of Christ can bring freedom to all captives. And let us be thankful for being able to praise God from deep within our souls so that we might be a living testimony for others. May it be so. **AMEN.**

PRAYER

Holy Son of God, save us, restore us, and lead us in the way of your grace and peace. Help us to hold dear your promise of love into the world. Amen.

Birthing a Promise

What does the promised birth of Jesus Christ mean for us today?

Sunday, December 20, 2020
Fourth Sunday of Advent

Birthing a Promise
On this last Sunday of Advent, and with only four days before Christmas, Luke's gospel shares the story of the angel Gabriel, who came to tell Mary that she will birth a **promise of God's love.** As the angel Gabriel shared with Mary to name her baby Jesus, who is to be called the Holy, Son of God! [122]

And so, with a heart of gratitude for this holy birth, we may ask, **"What does the promised birth of Jesus Christ mean for us today?"**

As Gabriel's message, first, confirms God's faithful promise of Christ's coming, and secondly, it shows us that God is always with us.

As it is important to note, earlier in the story, before the angel Gabriel came to Mary, he also appeared to Zechariah, the wife of Mary's cousin, Elizabeth, to tell him that he and Elizabeth would have a son.

But, to truly get the significance of what was said by the angel Gabriel, we are to be reminded that Zechariah and Elizabeth were beyond the normal range for bearing children, when the angel said, 'And you will give birth to a son, and he will prepare the way for the Messiah.' [123]

And so, today, the story of God is among us, continues, as we hear how the angel Gabriel comes to Mary to tell Mary that she would become pregnant and give birth to the Son of God. And, of course, Mary was amazed by this divine birth that would bear witness to God's love for all people.

Yet, this news was more than just an earthly kind of news; it was a divine blessing. It was something that would excite both Mary and Joseph, realizing that it was God's voice of birthing a promise of eternal love. It was something that only God could do and has, indeed, done. And that is why, we heard in our scripture reading, that 'nothing is impossible with God.' [124]

Mary is very excited about receiving the Good News of this divine birth and could not keep the excitement to herself. So, she walks over to Elizabeth's home and shares the news with her. And we're told in Luke 1:41, NIV, "[that] when Elizabeth heard Mary's greeting, the baby leaped in her womb, and Elizabeth was filled with the Holy Spirit."

And in response to being filled with the Holy Spirit, Elizabeth says in Luke 1:42, NIV, "Blessed are you among women, and blessed is the child (the fruit of your womb) you will bear!"

A modern-day example of taking comfort in a promise is in a story of a little girl named Rachel. [125] Rachel was a preschooler who was afraid to sleep alone and, as a result, would crawl into bed with her parents. But, there came a time when Rachel's mom had to travel for work, and her dad came up with an idea, which was to sleep in the spare bunk bed in her room.

Rachel thought it was a great idea. So, that night, Rachel went to sleep on time. And a couple of hours later, when her dad crawled into the top bunk, she was sound asleep. And she slept like that all night.

The following day, Rachel told her dad that she slept through the night because he was in the room. But her dad saw that Rachel was asleep when he came into the room, and so he asked, 'How did you know I was there?'

And Rachel answered, 'Because you said you would be there.'

This story reminds us that God keeps promises and loves us like loving parents.

And now, let us return to our question, **"What does the promised birth of Jesus Christ mean for us today?"**

The scriptures reveal that God's loving promise to be with us and comfort us is for everyone because we are all children of God. And, the coming of Jesus Christ reveals that we are also to 'bear witness' [126] to God's love coming into the world.

Trusting in God's promise to love us is what it takes to bear witness to God's activity in the world, which leads us to resist injustice, fear, and doubt by trusting in God's promise for a better world filled with divine love.

This is the kind of love that the prophet Nathan spoke of in our Old Testament reading today as we hear of God's forgiveness towards people who struggle with issues of morality. And in response, the people bear witness to the active unconditional love of God.

We also see that Mary' bears witness' to God's actions of unconditional love birthed for all of humanity. As Mary celebrates the anticipation of Jesus Christ in her song in today's Gospel reading, which is popularly known, as the Magnificat and is translated as 'the one who glorifies or magnifies' and is the first Christmas song ever sung. It reflects her faith. A faith that believed God loves everyone. As Mary bears witness to the kind of faith that believes God could even love an ordinary person, like herself.

And when we reflect upon Christ's birth, we, like Mary, also sing, to the glory of the Lord! As we sing about the angels who were messengers of

God's promise. We sing carols of great cheer that remind us of the hope, peace, joy, and love that came at Christmas.

We continue Mary's Magnificat with each song sung to glorify Christ's birth! And it has been our tradition to 'bear witness to God's love on Earth, during our Christmas Eve candlelight services. Because this is the time when we glorify the Lord by bearing witness through song, in a variety of musical selections about Christ's love, as the choir would sing anthems, and all sing several songs in celebration of our Savior's birth!

And one of the things that we would typically do on this Sunday of every year is go caroling to our sick and shut-in church family members and friends. And we would do this because we feel that it is essential to think about the gifts that we will receive, but we also consider the many ways we can give. And caroling has been one of those beautiful ways we can give back to our friends and others who enjoy our visits! We can continue singing and bearing witness to God's promise in reimagined ways such as virtual worship like we are doing today and safe distancing outdoors like we plan to do on Christmas Eve.

The Magnificat celebrates the message shared with all of humanity, which is to help us to see that we all bear Christ in some meaningful way. In that, God has a purpose for each of us. And we are to give birth to it so that we can receive the blessings that God has purposed for us so that we will be able to share our gifts with others.

And in our doing so, we might experience the love of God who sent Jesus Christ to come into the world as an infant holy. So that we would share the unconditional love of God, whose plan is for us to love with a heart that entirely seeks to unite us all together by opening our hearts to 'bear witness' to God's loving presence in our daily living.

Jesus Christ is our living, breathing sign of the immeasurable love that God has had for all of us from the very beginning. Christ is the living promise that we are never, ever, alone. Because regardless of where we are in life, what condition we find ourselves in, or how far we might stray away from God, who is supreme in love, will never leave us alone. It is a love that never stops shining and guiding us upward and onward. Now, that is Magnificat! Or, as the young folks say, that is lit!!

And so, let us be like Mary and 'bear witness' to God's birthing promise, which comforts us through our fears, our griefs, and our hardships. Let us be like the prophet Nathan and 'bear witness' to God's birthing promise, which loves us unconditionally. And let us' bear witness' to God's birthing promise, which asks everyone to bring justice, mercy, and peace of Jesus Christ into the world. May it be so, now and always. **Amen.**

PRAYER

God of grace, we rejoice that you choose to dwell among us. Fill us with your Spirit that we may hear the announcement of Jesus' coming birth and proclaim the good news of your promises fulfilled. AMEN.

LETTER THIRTY-SEVEN

Christmas Eve Reflection

Thursday, December 24, 2020
THE GOOD NEWS ON CHRISTMAS EVE

CHRISTMAS EVE REFLECTION: The Light of Christ
This evening, we have come to adore the Christ Child, whose loving light shines throughout the world. For it is written:
A child has been born for us,
a son is given to us;
authority rests upon his shoulders;
and he is named
Wonderful Counselor, Mighty God,
Everlasting Father, Prince of Peace.

The birth of the Christ Child is the fulfillment of God's loving promise to be with us and among us in every season of our lives, especially in those seasons of despair. In that, God offers us Christ's guiding light, even in the midst, of the darkest night!

And in celebration of the Christ-Child's birth, we have paused for a moment to praise God's love and light through reading sacred scriptures and singing sacred songs that remind us of Christ's heavenly light that is shining brightly upon us all!

As we proclaim the wonder of God incarnate, being with us, through the birth of Jesus Christ, who has come into the troubled world, to offer redemption and loving grace, to everyone!

And to show our love and appreciation for all that God has done year after year, we sing, O Come All Ye Faithful, joyful and triumphant!! As we welcome one another into this sacred space to remember Bethlehem, the place where Christ was born. And we joyfully sing in adoration, to the Christ Child, who comes to us, as a child, bringing hope, peace, joy, love, and light to shine in each of our lives!

As our long-awaited gift, of the Christ Child, has indeed arrived! And on this night, the people of God hear the Heavenly choir singing loudly. We hear the Heavenly choir singing with joy because the people around Him had been in mourning on the night of Jesus Christ's birth. They were in lonely exile because they were without their land. And they waited in expectation for the glory of God to appear on earth to help light the path towards their freedom.

And that is why we hear from the scripture that the coming of the Christ Child causes the gloomy clouds of night and sadness to go away. The light from God shines brightly so that we all might be led to the Christ Child. In that, the light of God's Beloved Child offers to humanity a sweet melody of peace that calls for all nations, and all people, to be bound together with one heart and with one mind.

The scriptures remind us that it is from dust, that God has breathed life into every one of us, and it is the same God who will deliver us from earthly bondage, sadness, and conflict. For on this night, we hear about the coming of the Christ Child, and we cannot help but sing about this beautiful Child!! This Child is so lowly, meek, and mild. This Child brings new life, hope, and joy to all!! As we listen to come together, singing 'Glory, to the newborn King!!' [127]

Many of us need the newness of life. This year has brought about so much change, and along with it, grief. And so, we need Christ's light to shine even deeper within our hearts because many of us are broken, hurt, alone, or sad. And yet, even during our sorrow, the Christ Child reminds us of God's steadfast love and light, which guides us and comforts us in our struggles and revives us to help us get through tomorrow with more ease.

The Christ Child shines on this night as the Prince of Peace and the One who brings justice because He brings healing light to all!! As Jesus Christ, born of the Virgin Mary, is God's gift, of unconditional love and light, to all the world, at Christmas, and for all eternity!

And so, as we receive the light of the Christ Child in our hearts, let us not only anticipate the 'sounds' of wrapping paper being ripped apart on Christmas morning but let us also remember the 'sounds' of singing at Christmas in celebration of the Christ Child. Let us also hear the 'sounds' of Christ's mercy. Let us hear the 'sounds' of Christ's peace. Let us hear the 'sounds' of Christ's equal justice. Let us hear the 'sounds' of Christ's forgiving grace. Let us hear the 'sounds' of hope. Let us hear the 'sounds' of new joy. And most of all, let us listen to the 'quiet sound' of that silent night, which reminds us of the reason for the season, which is to pause and be grateful for God's gift of the Christ Child, and to follow His light by being Sunbursts of lights to everyone, everywhere. May it be so. **Amen.**

CHAPTER FOUR

THE CHRISTMAS AND
EPIPHANY SEASONS

During this season, the U.S. announces coronavirus vaccines for wider distribution. This season was also met with a televised rally in front of the White House vigorously contesting the election, which later concluded with the world watching in shock and horror, an insurrection at the U.S. Capitol by the outgoing president's supporters who sought to overturn the national election by brutal force. However, the world would also witness the peaceful transition of power held at the U.S. Capitol during the inauguration of President Joe Biden and Vice President Kamala Harris. The State of Georgia would also land historic wins, sending two minorities to the U.S. Senate.

PRAYER

Ever-faithful God, through your Word, you promised to establish a household of peace through justice. [128] Open our hearts to receive your Son that we may continue to welcome all people into this household of faith. Amen.

LETTER THIRTY-EIGHT

Long-Awaited Gift

What does the long-awaited gift of Christ's birth mean for us today?

Sunday, December 27, 2020
First Sunday after Christmas

Long-Awaited Gift
Friends, the Christ Child has come! On this first Sunday after Christmas, Luke's gospel shares the story of the **long-awaited gift**, Baby Jesus. He came to offer a blessing of new beginnings not only to Mary and Joseph to raise as their newborn baby, but whose love came from God to provide a blessing of new beginnings for all of God's children!!

And so, with a heart of gratitude for Christ's birth, we may ask, **"What does the long-awaited gift of Christ's birth mean for us today?"**

As we can look at today's message that first confirms the faithfulness of God through Christ's birth which secondly calls upon us to recognize that we are all sons and daughters of God.

And today's scripture lesson examples God's loving faithfulness as we hear the prophet Isaiah rejoicing in the Lord for shining down on Jerusalem for the sake of justice and equality, likening it to the burning bush that God uses to speak with Moses. And we also hear of God's loving faithfulness from the psalmist who offers praises to God and tells all of creation to praise our Creating, God. And then, Luke builds upon God's loving faithfulness as we learn about Anna, the devoted prophetess who breaks into an anthem of praise to God when she sees that the long-awaited gift has arrived!

Christ's birth examples a new beginning and is indeed a blessing as Luke gives us details of how Mary and Joseph follow the ancient Jewish ritual of blessing, which goes back to the days of Moses and recognizes that all children are a gift from God.

Now, let us return to our question, **"What does the long-awaited gift of Christ's birth mean for us today?"**

We are to be like those early believers praising God for what is and praising God for what is to come!! Because of God's loving faithfulness in the long-awaited gift of Jesus Christ confirming that God indeed loves us all!

And we, along with our wider church, declare ourselves to be on a journey to be the love that Christ as we work to build a just world for all.

Our three great loves are the love of children, neighbor, and creation.

How many of us love our children here at Union? We demonstrate our love for children by the way we incorporate our children into morning worship and by offering them Christian education week after week. But in addition to showing love for the children at Union, we also show love for children by our standing on the side of justice that calls for children to get a second chance when they commit minor offenses.

How many of us would say we love our neighbor? As we demonstrate our love of neighbor by how we serve one another. In that, we support one another in so many ways. We offer words of comfort, we offer the peace of Christ, and we do what we can to help our friends in need. But we also reach beyond these walls as we support the immigrant family who works on the farm to get us food. We help with providing food for the family who we call the working poor because the cost of living is rising at a higher rate than the working wages even though the working-class family serves our everyday needs.

And how many of us would say that we love God's creation? As we seek to embrace the welcoming message of loving all of God's creation when we say week after week, no matter who you are or where you are on God's journey, you are welcome here. We not only welcome those who walk through the doors of this household of God's justice and peace. Week after week, we also welcome God's creations who are homeless and in need of a place for their families to find temporary rest when financial hardships have come their way.

The message for today speaks to God's loving faithfulness of new beginnings through the Christ-Child. And we example our hearts opening to new faces by the way we offer new life by loving the children by the way we provide new life by living our neighbor and by the way we love all of God's creation.

And that is why we can join in singing praises to God for what is and what is to come because we know that God sent His Son, Jesus. He came to love. He came to heal, and He came to forgive.

Therefore, we can sing praises because joy has come into the world. And we are asked that every heart prepare room for Christ to enter in. And we can sing praises like the prophets and the heavenly choir because the Christ-Child rules the world with truth and light even in our waiting.

There are times when we must wait on God like a child stays to see what is under the tree on Christmas morning. In that, we trust that God knows what we need, but we await anxiously for the gift that we expect to come.

Many of us have struggled with patience. As waiting is our challenge, we are to be reminded by our faith that there are fresh possibilities right here in front of us. In that, we all belong to God because we are all of God's children. And the scripture tells us that whatever it is that we need, God has already provided a way for us to receive it, but we will receive it in God's timing as exampled in the long-awaited gift of the Christ-Child.

We behold the Christ-Child. We aim to be like Christ in the world so that we can indeed be the church that loves in the ways of Christ. And therefore, we are called to go out into the world doing our best to tell others of God's loving grace and immeasurable love that God has had for us all from the very beginning now and for all eternity.

As God's love and light continue to break forth in new beginnings and unexpected ways. So, it is okay to wait for what God is purposed because in our waiting, we can still praise God for what is, and we can praise God for what is to come because God's ancient promise of love for all remains with us today as this hope of a new beginning is present in the birth and the life of Jesus Christ. **Amen.**

PRAYER

Guiding God, your light beams into our lives, offering us hope. Help us hear your hope and draw nearer to you and your truth as we encounter your word together today. Amen.

LETTER THIRTY-NINE

Epiphany Celebration

How might we celebrate Christ's light in the New Year?

<u>Sunday, January 3, 2021</u>
<u>Second Sunday after Christmas</u>

Epiphany Celebration
In today's scripture lesson, all are to recognize, re-engage, and respond to the Christ Child's birth for the Epiphany celebration!

And in doing so, let us ask, **"How might we celebrate Christ's light in the new year?"**

The scriptures teach us that we are first to follow God's guiding light towards hope <u>so that we can, secondly, become shining lights of God's hope for the world.</u>

To understand the Epiphany story, we can look to Matthew's Gospel, in chapter 2, verses 1-12, which reminds us of the three wise men. They traveled from the East and were likely scholars with years of experience studying the ancient scriptures and had a good sense of astrology.

But, more importantly, their travels from such far places speak to the ways that God's love and light shine throughout the world. As these kings, who were from afar, followed the long-awaited, guiding light that led them to the Christ Child, who was born, the King of kings and whose love and light continues to reign supreme, for us all.

The kings who traveled from different far-away places were excited to follow the guiding light. The light revealed the time had come for renewed hope to be born into the world, hope that embraces all people into God's marvelous light, hope that shines upon all of humanity so that we all might become united in God's love and light.

And it is with this hope the three wise ones celebrated the Christ Child and were eager to go, tell it to others!! Yes, they told others of God's love and light, over the hills and everywhere!!

Now, let us return to our question, **"How might we celebrate Christ's light in the new year?"**

We can celebrate Christ's love and light by continuing to offer ourselves as Christ's love and light for a more peaceful and just-filled world. In that, we celebrate the Epiphany, like the three wise ones, who traveled from different places, and were guided by God to the Christ Child because hope was given freely to us all!

As we, who are worshipping virtually, or worshipping in the sanctuary and seated, six feet apart like the wise ones, are from many different places, and yet, we have come together, united to celebrate Christ's love and light. We have come together, united to celebrate the birth of the Christ Child, who offers hope to us still.

And for these reasons, some two thousand years later, we continue to celebrate on the 12th day of Christmas, which is January 6, and the day of Epiphany. We celebrate because we still embrace the new hope of the Christ Child, whose birth saves and heals the world from its hopelessness and despair.

As we, the church, are like those wise men, who are following the light of Christ to heal us from the hopelessness and despair in the world and to then, be able to 'go, tell it,' [129] to others near and far!

And yet, before we go and tell of the love of God, we are to follow God prayerfully. The story of the three wise men concludes by notifying us that after the Epiphany celebration, the three wise ones had a dream that they should take a different route, back to their respective homes. They did as God's dream instructed them to do, and they arrived safely at their homes.

And so, for a moment, let us recognize, re-engage, and respond to our journey through 2020 and into 2021.

It is safe to say that 2020 will be one for the record books as one memorable journey that needed the saving and healing of the Christ Child's love and light. In that, we recognize, now more than ever, that we need God's presence to be among us. God did not speak to us in a dream, a whisper, or even a shout. God shook us to our very core. In that, we dealt with deadly viruses that called for change whether we wanted to or not. One virus is a coronavirus, and the other is systemic racism.

The virus changed travel plans. The way we worship changed. The way kids learned at school changed. The ways we entertain ourselves, by watching sporting events, attending live concerts, gathering with loved ones, or just hanging out at our favorite restaurant changed. So much changed!

Not only did we have to recognize the need for change, but we also had to re-engage and respond to these unexpected changes. And unfortunately, we did not do as the wise ones did after the Epiphany celebration and unite in changing course as needed.

Some of us re-engaged by coming together and supporting people of color in ways they had never done before. Many systemic entities were vowing to commit to ending racism in the workplace and criminal justice systems throughout the nation. And some grassroots efforts took to the streets with peaceful marches that called for 'Black Lives to Matter," too.

Some of us found to re-engage and responded by choosing not to follow the guidelines from the coronavirus experts. And, not all of us wore masks, nor did we change our physical distancing when we interacted with others.

And as a result, the death toll in 2020 climbed to more than 300,000 deaths from the coronavirus alone.

We became tired and uncertain with such change, and those who hoped for unity became doubtful. And as we approached the New Year, we, as a church, thought of how best to become energized. We focused on uniting as a church, on the election, by educating and encouraging all to 'get out the vote.' [130]

We also united, as a church, in recognizing the massive deaths and losses of 2020, so we participated in three nationwide vigils to mourn our losses. Some of us offered leadership at the vigils.

WHAT A JOURNEY 2020 was for us, and praise God, we made it this far! We have landed in 2021 and celebrate the Epiphany because Christ's love and light are still with us. And, like the wise ones who saw God's love and light revealed, we cannot go back the same way we came. We take a new route home. As we are taught in the scripture, to be firm in our faith, and embrace, a new hope!!!

As the Epiphany is the celebration of God's love and the light shown to us through the Christ Child and God's love is with us, still. And so, we can embrace new hope as we journey into 2021, together, united as the church of Jesus Christ.

Like the wise ones, we can celebrate and take on the new routes with faith and new resolve, that we are not on this journey alone because God is with us. We will prayerfully become closer to God and be comforted by the words of the prophet Jeremiah. His words console us as we sing and raise shouts of joy in the future promise of hope, found in our saving and healing, Christ.

The scripture reveals that the Christ Child is not born to lead one group of people, but indeed, sent to guide us all. And because of this, we can travel into the New Year with renewed hope, recognizing, re-engaging, and responding united under God's love and light.

As the renewed hope and resolve of God's love for each of us leads us through our grief and our suffering and gives us the courage to continue onward into peace, comfort, and joy!

And so, let us celebrate this Epiphany as a symbol of God's love with hope. Let us also be comforted by the Christ Child, who is God-given, world-defying, wound-healing, and soul-saving.

And let us go out and tell of the peace, hope, joy, and love found in drawing closer with God, whose presence brings us to singing! May it be so. **Amen.**

PRAYER

Renewing God, your eternal love is shown through Jesus Christ. Help us strengthen our relationship with You and one another as we encounter your Word together. Amen.

LETTER FORTY

Defining Moments

How might the defining moments of Christ's baptism offer us a fresh start?

<u>Sunday, January 10, 2021</u>
The Baptism of Christ

DEFINING MOMENTS
On this Baptism of Christ Sunday, we learn about the defining moments that occurred at Jesus' baptism as the sky bursts open and the Spirit of God is revealed!

And, with this sense of wonder, we ask, **"How might the defining moments of Christ's baptism offer to us a new identity and a fresh start?"**

As Christ's baptism shows us that we are to <u>1) realize that God's promised change will come, and 2) trust that God's eternal love and light offers to guide us, still.</u>

And so, as we reflect upon God's defining moments in our Gospel lesson for today, we find that John the Baptizer offered believers the hope that God had not forgotten about them.

In that, we hear the voice of John the Baptizer crying out in the wilderness saying, "Repent, for the Kingdom of Heaven is at hand." [131] John's voice brought a crowd of diverse people from the city and village who listened to these words. We hear those with different religious views, such as the Pharisees and Sadducees, along with the soldiers and tax collectors, the rich and poor, including men and women. Even in their differences, they met on common ground in anticipation of a deliverer who would advocate on their behalf.

Heard in the wilderness was John's loud and clear cry for a healing savior, which was only a few hours away from Jerusalem. John's voice also traveled upward along the winding Jordan River. And as a result, growing numbers came to the banks of that sacred river. Some came to inquire, and some came to see, while others came to be baptized. And this is the place where we enter the scene for this morning's reading.

Jesus' baptism occurs when He comes forward and stands before the people. And then, following His baptism, we hear the Spirit-voice of God proclaiming that Jesus is the Son of God. And for all who witnessed the great baptism of Jesus Christ, they were blessed to experience what John had preached about as these defining moments of Christ's baptism had changed their lives forever because they saw that the Spirit of God was amongst them.

Let us now return to our question, **"How might the defining moments of Christ's baptism offer us a new identity and a fresh start?"**

The sacred act of Christ's baptism reminds us that we all belong to God and that God loves us regardless of what happens or how discouraged we might feel. And Christ's baptism also reveals to us that regardless of what is happening around us, God's love and light are with us in every circumstance and every changing season of life.

And, we see the changing season in the life of Jesus Christ, occurring after His baptism as it is essential to note that before Christ's baptism, Jesus, for the most part, kept a low profile. He was not out preaching, performing miracles, or confronting those religious leaders who did not show equal justice for all people.

And yet, we see in today's lesson; the time had come for Jesus Christ to do His divine work. His baptism marked the beginning of Jesus Christ's public ministry.

As God's love through baptism is like the loving story about the 99 sheep, the Gospel of Luke 15:4, NIV, tells of the one sheep, who was lost... as the shepherd leaves the 99 sheep and goes to find the one, lost sheep. As this message tells us, even the lost sheep was important to the shepherd and its community.

And so, when it comes to Jesus' baptism, the Scripture affirms God's commitment to love us, not some of us but all of us, and calls upon us to do the same.

And that is why the Word of God in Isaiah 43:1b, 4a, NRSV, says, "Do not fear, for I have redeemed you; I have called you by name, you are mine... you are precious in my sight, and honored, and I love you." And then, goes on to say, "I have inscribed you on the palms of my hands" (Isaiah 49:16, NRSV).

This message of God's love for us is in a picture I read about an old burned-out mountain shack. And all that remained was the chimney with the charred debris of what had been that family's sole possession. In front of this destroyed home stood an older man dressed only in his underclothes with a small boy clutching a pair of patched overalls. And it was evident that the child was crying.

Beneath the picture were the words that the artist seemed to have felt. The older man was saying to the boy. They were simple words, yet, they presented a profound theology and philosophy of life. Those words were, "Hush child, God, ain't dead!" [132]

Beloved many of us are like that scared little boy crying because we feel that God has somehow become absent and has taken away the joy from our lives. As we, like the little boy, can look at the events of this past week and recall the thrill of democracy being celebrated, with more than four million Georgians voting and thus, making history with the first African-American. First, Jewish Americans to serve in the U.S. Senate from the State of Georgia!!

And yet, like that little boy in the painting, we felt heartbreak on that day of historical celebration. Our joy turned into tears while watching our democracy burn. There was a fire of hatred in the hearts of our fellow neighbors. They convened from near and far as our U.S. Capitol was under seized by a mobocracy, that also made history in the most undemocratic of ways. And we, like the crying child in the photo, can also be comforted by the words, that 'God is not dead!' As we can trust that God is alive and shining a light of hope for us all, even in the darkest of nights.

Today, the Genesis scripture reminds us that God is our creator and is still creating. In that, God names the darkness night, and the light is day as God creates something out of nothing and makes all things new. And we see God making the ordinary extraordinary in the creation story, and Christ's baptism as God's Spirit-voice speaks and reminds us that we are to live amongst one another, equally, as children of God's beloved creation.

As Christ's baptism connects to all believers, which means we can all receive newness of life. It is freely given to us by the Spirit of God! This newness of life opens our hearts to shed new light on old questions about who we are and how we behave. Our journey into this new season of the Epiphany can help strengthen the hope that God has for us to shine the Christ light in our lives and advocate for equitable love for everyone.

Baptism is hope and comfort to those who have Christ in their hearts and is also available to those still searching. And that is why today's psalmist affirms God's love, by singing that the 'voice of God is full of majesty,[133] in that, God's voice is over the waters God's voice is powerful, and God's voice gives strength to the people.

All are welcome to see the Child of God, who came to live amongst humanity. As Christ came for all to believe in the fulfilled promises of

God and to unite with Him in Baptism, as the beloved children of God so that we all might witness the amazing grace of God's love and justice by hearing, with fresh ears, God's voice speaking to our hearts, to help ease our fears. Because the great and glorious light, witnessed at the birth, and baptism of Jesus Christ, remind us that God's promises are for all whom God created, formed, and made, which includes everyone, everywhere.

And so, let our wounded hearts open to the healing waters of Christ's baptism. Let our troubled souls open to the guiding light of Christ's baptism. Let us allow God's love to be evident in who we are and how we behave. And let us share the defining moments of Christ's baptism with others so that all might know of God's eternal love and light that guides us along the way. May it be so. **Amen.**

PRAYER

Loving God, as you called the first disciples from their daily work, you also call us in our everyday life. Help us to hear your voice and to discern your call. And strengthen us as we learn to share your message of justice and peace. Amen.

LETTER FORTY-ONE

Known and Loved

How might God's role in our lives impact others?

Sunday, January 17, 2021
Second Sunday after Epiphany

KNOWN AND LOVED
In each of today's readings, God's call is towards something more significant than we know. The scriptures suggest that we are all **known and loved** by God, and we are to be God's light in the world.

And, we ask, **"How might God's role in our lives impact others?"**

The scriptures suggest that when we <u>first seek to discern how God is speaking to us, we can live into the purpose, meaning, and call that God has upon our lives.</u>

Today, we learn about the remarkable story of how Samuel makes the transition from childhood to his becoming a prophet. We see how God speaks to Samuel, [134] and how God, ultimately, speaks through Samuel. In that, the call Samuel receives from God does not only impact him spiritually; it affects the way he lives. And as a result, Samuel's community was transformed by Godly love, both socially and politically.

Sheila Harvey

Now, let us return to the question, **"How might God's role in our lives impact others?"**

As we, like Samuel, can continue listening to the role has for our lives, the church, and the ways that we will be used to transform other lives through acts of Godly love.

Our Gospel reading in John today teaches us not to dismiss another person because of their background. We are not to ignore a person because of their religion. We are not to dismiss a person because of their economic status, and we are not to dismiss anyone based on the distinctions we make about those around us.

In that, on this Sunday, when we honor God's incredible calling upon the life of the Rev. Dr. Martin Luther King, Jr, we see the similarity of Samuel's story to that of Dr. King's story. Both were raised to believe in God and later received a calling from God to lead a peace and justice movement that helped transform an entire nation.

God's call upon our lives directly impacts the lives of others because God's calling reminds us that all of creation is known and loved by God. This kind of hopeful visioning is at the heart of the famous "I Have a Dream" speech made by Dr. King that we heard together during our time of prayer.

Hearing this speech again reminds me of being at the anniversary of the March on Washington last summer, on August 28, when tens of thousands of people were standing in unity, gathered together for justice, and marching in peace.

Being at the March of Washington brought forth a great appreciation for all the efforts made by those civil rights workers, faith communities, and supporters who risked so much by seeking justice while remaining peaceful and helping shine a light on racial and economic inequalities.

As the anniversary of the March on Washington reminded us we have come such a long way as Rev. Al Sharpton stated that the first time he went to the march on Washington, a little white girl spat on him, and during last year's March on Washington, a little white girl told him, NO JUSTICE, NO PEACE! As MLK's granddaughter would later stand on the stage and represent the hopeful future of unity.

In that, the greatest commandment in the Bible teaches us to love one another as God loves us because we are all created by God, as the beloved community. And yet, there are false teachings that are not of God. They teach that God created a select group over another, which is not the teaching of Jesus Christ.

But, when false religious teachers arise, our hearts should ache because of the ministers and churchgoers involved in inciting hatred on social media. Our hearts should ache because of the ministers and churchgoers engaged in the violent insurrection at the U.S. Capitol. Our hearts should ache because of the 'good people' who quietly allow the rhetoric of hatred and untruths in your presence or on our social media.

It is tempting to respond to God's call to love by saying, 'there is nothing I can do.' But, here is something we can do when our friends and loved ones are not showing love to others. We can shine Christ's light by saying to our friends and loved ones that 'God is calling us to love one another as we love ourselves, therefore, I love you, and I love the others, too.' [135] We could say to our friends and loved ones that 'the same God who created me, created you and God, created, the others, too.' In short, we can say to those we know and love, who are spreading acts of hate, that it is our Christian duty to show acts of love to every neighbor, everywhere.

And by doing so, we will continue growing in Godly love, which is in the words of Dr. King, who reminds us about the teachings of justice and peace from the King of Kings, our Lord, and Savior, Jesus the Christ! The 'I Have a Dream' speech offered by Dr. King highlights God's call for us all to show love for one another.

Friends, we are actively acting in love so that the dream of equality, peace, and justice for all people will become a reality one day. Like the scriptures, today calls for us to **wake up** and know our privilege and worth!! We are to hold each other accountable for how we love each other. As the Good

News is that God knows and loves us all. Rich, working-class, and poor. Different races, gender, and generation. Every religious, non-religious, and cult follower. Yup, Jesus Christ has challenged us to wake up, and act in love towards everyone, everywhere.

And so, let God's challenge of peace, justice, and love begin with each of us, right now by saying in the mirror or writing virtually to everyone 'the peace of Christ is in you.' Let us also be healers and truth-tellers. And let us join, with each of our hearts, in peace. May it be so. **Amen.**

PRAYER

Persistent God, you called the fishers from their daily work, and you call us during everyday life. Help us to hear your voice and to discern Your call. And strengthen us as we learn to share the message of your love for equal justice and peace. Amen.

LETTER FORTY-TWO

Follow Me

In what ways is God calling us to move into a new future?

Sunday, January 24, 2021
Third Sunday after Epiphany

FOLLOW ME
In today's gospel lesson, we learn that Jesus is beginning his public ministry, and while traveling along the Sea of Galilee, He says to four fishermen, 'Come, follow Me.' [136] Then, they immediately stopped what they were doing and became the first followers of Jesus Christ.

And so, let us ask, **"In what ways is God calling us to move into this new future?"**

The scripture encourages us first to accept Christ's invitation for a deeper relationship with Him to receive a renewed sense of purpose for our lives.

To get an idea of God calling us into a new season for our lives, let us look to Jonah, who spent an entire day walking across the city of Nineveh that generally, would typically have, taken three days to walk across.

As we see that God spoke to Jonah with a sense of urgency about not being able to ignore Nineveh's evil treatment of one another any longer. [137]

251

And so, Jonah listens to God, gets up, and immediately walks to the city of Nineveh. We learn that Jonah walks through this city for an entire day, delivering the message of repentance to everyone by preaching that they stop treating each other poorly. In following God's call, we see that Jonah had a renewed sense of purpose as he walked through Nineveh that day. We hear in the story Jonah could have walked along the outskirts of the city, which would have been safer for him, and in the event, the people did not like what Jonah preached, he could have gotten out of that city in a hurry. And yet, if he had gone this route, it would have taken Jonah three days to get through Nineveh.

But instead, Jonah allows God to use him as an urgent messenger, to turn the people around and work. The people of Nineveh believed and asked for God's forgiveness. They changed their bad behavior, and their city was saved because they answered God's call for them to love one another.

We also hear about God's love for everyone everywhere in today's psalm. The psalmist calls upon all believers to pour out their hearts to God and wait with hope by trusting that God will speak and deliver everyone from evil.

We see that Jonah and the Psalmist have a message of resilience, recovery, and renewal for all people, which prepares us for Mark's life-changing message as we hear Jesus speaking to four fishermen Andrew, Simon, James, and John. He calls upon them to immediately change their established identities and follow Him.

And when Jesus invited them to change from their everyday routine, they chose to discover God in a new way, all of them. As they immediately dropped everything to follow Jesus.

Now, let us return to our question, **"How is God calling us to move into a new future?"**

Well, it is clear from scripture that God is calling upon all of humanity to open our hearts and to show acts of love for God, ourselves, and one another. Like the stories we heard today, God calls upon us to follow, with a sense of renewed purpose and with a sense of commitment on how to treat each other better. That is why Jesus says, to us all, 'Follow me.' [138]

Jesus reaches us right where we are and speaks our language, just as He did with those fishermen. And that is why Jesus said, "Follow me, and I will make you fishers of people." [139] And they would become fishers of people to fill all with the Good News of God's love.

They would become good fishers by sharing with others that Jesus not only calls us to a life of urgency and conviction, but Jesus also calls us to a task to show love. As Jesus calls us to give others what he has first given us- love, caring, and forgiveness.

It seems that following Jesus Christ is needed now as they needed it then. In that, sharing the love of God still offers hope in a hurting world.

Sharing God's love is indeed urgent, at every time and place. We heard God tell Jonah to preach with urgency, for the people to change from being evil to one another, and to show their love for God and one another by repenting.

We also saw the urgency of the psalmist to spread God's love by sharing that we are to wait with great anticipation in silence so that our worrying would cease, and God's voice could fill the air so that we can receive a renewed sense of purpose.

Mark's Gospel begins with John's arrest. And with urgency, we hear Jesus preaching that the 'Time is up.' At that moment, those four fishermen chose to engage in a deeper relationship with God and share the urgency of the Good News being someone better by loving others.

And this old legend that I heard some time ago is another example of Godly love through sharing as the story begins talking about a devout and generous man who has recently died. And, before he goes through the Pearly Gates, he requested first to take one peek at Hell. And at the Gateway of Hell, he was astounded to see long tables filled with food that looked scrumptious. And then, he saw multitudes of people who poured into the room, and they looked starved, almost like skeletons.

And fastened to each person's forearm were yard-long, forks and spoons. He observed as they frantically fought to feed themselves, but it was in vain. And it truly looked like a living, Hell.

Back in Heaven, the man saw tables similarly set up. When the Heavenly host came in, he saw that the people there also had each of their forearms fastened with a yard-long fork and spoon, but the difference was he saw that when they sat down instead of trying to feed themselves, they began to feed each other. Then, the new resident knew it was Heaven.

Sharing is what we do. It is the sign that marks the life of a follower of Jesus. Sharing our faith, sharing our resources, sharing a part of ourselves with others is the urgency of this Christian life.

Jesus calls us to love the ones in this world that nobody else will love. Jesus calls us to reach out to the lonely, the hungry, the sick, the differently-abled, the forsaken, and to all those people who need to hear that someone indeed does love them. And that includes us, too! As each of us is to be someone who will follow in the ways of Christian love.

To love is not always easy. It requires us to follow in the prophet's ways, Micah, who tells us to love justice, love kindness, and walk humbly with God. In that, love is an action word. Love calls upon us to do something. Love calls upon us to trust God in everything. Love calls upon us to do the hard work of equal justice in non-violent ways.

We are like the people we read about in the bible today in so many ways. We are to change our practices as a nation urgently and to become more loving towards one another. We are to urgently change our mindset that puts money first to put people first. We are to imagine something completely new so that systemic injustices would turn into the hopes and dreams of so many who have responded to God's urgent call that unites humanity so that there is equal justice for all.

During our bible study discussions last week, we could not help but speak of how God is speaking to our nation by calling us to move forward in love. And to prayerfully communicate this message of showing acts of love, more broadly, so that others might know that THIS is the Good News message of Jesus Christ and not evil actions that illuminate hate.

And so, let us imagine something new that could change the world with our love. Let us imagine a new way of communicating amongst ourselves and within our larger society to have a peaceful and just-filled world for everyone, everywhere. And, let us continue to follow Jesus Christ by urgently sharing our loving actions so that all might experience God's love on earth, as it is in Heaven! May it be so. **Amen.**

PRAYER

God of our refuge and hope when the ways of this world divide us or when
we are in despair, comfort us so that we may be reminded of the power of
your inclusive love through Christ to whom we belong and in whom we
are one. Amen.

LETTER FORTY-THREE

Power to Do

How might we allow the power of God's love to cleanse our hearts and minds?

<u>Sunday, January 24, 2021</u>
<u>Third Sunday after Epiphany</u>

Power to Do
On this Fourth Sunday after the Epiphany, we listen to stories about God's **power to do** all things. As Jesus teaches and demonstrates His authority to drive away from an unclean heart so that every restless soul could experience peace by God's love.

And, we can ask, **"How might we allow the power of God's love to cleanse our hearts and minds?"**

The scriptures suggest that we <u>first seek God's loving guidance to help us in our despair so that we will secondly be able to offer kind words and healing acts of kindness towards ourselves and to one another.</u>

And that is why, in Deuteronomy, we hear that God's holy presence and power will indeed come and meet the needs of all people. Moses explains that God will send another prophet after him, who will come from amongst the people. This message was to encourage and support the exhausted preachers, who sought to continue their work of reminding others about

God's love. Moses further explains that God's faithful messenger will come surprisingly and speak God's words in God's name, and God will hold everyone accountable.

And in Mark's gospel story, we see that the prophetic message in Deuteronomy is fulfilled in the coming of Jesus Christ. Jesus surprises the people from within his community by teaching with divine authority. Jesus also was able to show his divinity when He healed an ill man possessed by an evil spirit.

The power of Jesus to teach with such authority, along with His good deeds of healing someone from having an unclean heart, disrupted the social norms. And we see that the social, political, and religious authorities decided to view Jesus as a blasphemer and revolutionary. But, the people in the synagogue who saw Jesus healing the man of the unclean spirit were amazed by the exorcism that they witnessed. They were even more amazed by the authority of Jesus.

Today's psalmist captures the heart of gratitude for God's great works. The psalm lists the miraculous ways that God shows up in our lives and nourishes us in our various cultural heritages so that we can have wisdom, be fair, and be respectful in the ways we care for one another.

Now, let us return to our question, **"How might we allow the power of God's love, to cleanse our hearts and minds?"**

In our response, we can trust that just like Jesus healed the ill man in the holy temple, God also has the power to heal us. God comes into our sacred temple, whether in the sanctuary or on live stream worship. God comes to cleanse our souls from any impure thought or action that seeks to harm another in any way.

And what is so exciting about being cleansed by God's love is that we can share this message of love with others in the way we live our lives.

An excellent example of this is passed along in an old story attributed to Gandhi. The story is about a mother who approached 'the Teacher' for assistance with a matter with her son. And she says, "My son has horrible eating habits. Please tell him to stop eating foods with so much sugar he will listen to you."

And after 'the Teacher' listened sympathetically, he says, "Please come back next week and make the request again."

So, the mother agrees and returns seven days later and says, "My son's problem continues, and I am very concerned about his health because he rarely eats vegetables or fruits." Then, she goes on to say to 'the teacher,' "please talk to him about the danger of overheating sugar."

And 'the teacher' says, "Please, come back and see me in a week."

And even though the mother was disappointed, she left and returned one week later. So, once again, she made her plea. But, this time, 'the Teacher' agreed to talk with her son.

And when the mother completed finished the conversation, she thanked 'the teacher' saying, "I am grateful that you took the time to talk to my son, but I just don't understand why it took three requests for you to do so."

And 'the teacher' looked at the mother and said, "I didn't realize how hard it would be for me to give up sugar."

As this story reminds us, all love builds up, and knowledge puffs up. In that, 'the teacher' exercised humility rather than superiority or arrogance. And by acting in love towards the son and his mother, 'the teacher' chose to practice what he was advising the son to do: give up sugar!

This story teaches us that when we speak with authority, we should humble our hearts and seek to live by what we say.

And like this story, Jesus also taught with authority and met with those who listened. Jesus spoke with a power rooted in love as His authority was not distant or top-heavy. It was born out of love for all people. In that, Jesus never requires his followers to do what he did not do.

Jesus Christ's teaching was different from that of any other teacher. Jesus based His teaching on love. The kind of love that placed no limits on reaching out to people from all walks of life. Jesus teaches us to have the kind of love that forgives, heals, frees, and accepts, even what society might classify as the worst of sinners and outcasts. In that, Jesus teaches us to have the kind of unconditional love that breaks down dividing walls and barriers of all kinds.

Jesus Christ is the authority of love whose human life was poured out on a cross for all humankind without distinctions showing acceptance of everyone.

And acceptance of everyone as the beloved community of God is lived out through our Health and Human Services Ministry. We see mental, spiritual, and physical health and wellness working together to support the whole person. And that is why we continue moving forward with an affordable senior housing mission for our church campus. Because we, like Jesus, understand that when one suffers, we all suffer.

This message of loving one another into healing and wholeness is the message of God's love. It is a message of equal justice. It is a message of peace being made possible. It is God's way of reaching into each of our hearts and cleansing us of our selfishness and our feeling entitled to live a lavish life while ignoring the poverty of someone crying out, in need of help, in times of despair.

It is difficult to speak the truth of loving ourselves and one another more deeply because we must live these truths ourselves. And, God knows, we are not perfect. But, the good news is that we can all call upon Jesus Christ, who is perfect in every way. And He has the power to cleanse us of every foul and evil thought that enters our hearts and minds.

And history has shown us, through Moses and Jesus, that when God's love cleanses us, we have the power to go out and get into 'good trouble,' like the late U.S. Congressman John Lewis.

One of the ways to get into 'good trouble' is to let others know the truth about God's equal love for everyone. In that, getting into 'good trouble' is telling the truth about the power of God to make the crooked places straight. Getting into 'good trouble' tells the truth so loudly and boldly and so often that it will overpower the BIG LIE of hate-filled narratives that fill the air on social media and at dinner tables. Getting into 'good trouble' helps us heal from all hopelessness of every evil spirit and reminds us about the power of God's loving and Holy Spirit, which guides us into doing and being better!

And so, when we are in despair, let us call upon our friend and savior, Jesus, who will meet us in our sacred spaces and give us rest. Our health or the health of our loved ones can cause us concern, so let us pray for Jesus to heal us into wholeness and give us rest.

And, when we are feeling less than perfect, let God's loving power of grace, mercy, hope, and abundance guide us to life everlasting. May it be so. **Amen.**

PRAYER

Holy One, you make all good things possible. Lift us when we are weary. Be our strength and fill us with hope as we seek to serve you and our neighbor this day. Amen.

LETTER FORTY-FOUR

Source of Strength

In what ways can God be the healing source of strength for us today?

Sunday, February 7, 2021
Fifth Day after Epiphany

Source of Strength
On this Women's Fellowship Sunday, Mark's Gospel speaks of Jesus Christ acting as the **source of strength** as Jesus emphasizes to all His followers the need to continue together in ministry to heal many others.

With this message to the disciples, our question might be, **"In what ways can God be the healing source of strength for us today?"**

The scripture suggests that <u>first, strength comes from our hope of being spiritually healed, which secondly guides how we serve God and one another.</u>

In preparation for this message about how being healed might impact others, I came across a story about a man who went to his doctor to ask if he could help him with his snoring problem. As soon as I go to sleep," the man explained, "I begin to snore. It happens all the time. What can I do, doctor, to cure myself?"

The doctor then asked, "Does it bother your wife?"

"Oh," the man answered, "it not only bothers her, but it disturbs the whole congregation." [140]

That doesn't happen with anyone here, of course!

But, this little story does have something to teach us about our gospel lesson today. Just as the man's snoring disturbed a whole congregation, Jesus' preaching and healing ministry also had a very profound impact on those who received the gospel message and healing by Jesus. This passage in Mark's gospel today allows us to learn about the healing work of Jesus.

It is no accident that the word "to heal" in the New Testament Greek also means "to save." Jesus saves people by healing them of physical, mental, emotional, and other diseases and illnesses. And in so doing, He demonstrates the power of God's love and hope for the world.

Mark tells us when the people of Capernaum got word of Jesus' message and works of healing, "the whole city was gathered around the door" of Simon Peter and Andrew's home. Jesus responds, "And he cured many who were sick with various diseases and cast out many demons." [141]

In Jesus' day, people commonly believed that evil spirits entered people's minds and bodies, thus suffering from mental illness and physical diseases. So, people thought of them as spiritually unclean. Jesus, as the Healer and Savior of the world, came to change all of that radically.

Jesus knew that the powers of evil function to hurt and divide human beings. Jesus came, he says in John's Gospel, that we human beings may have life and have it abundantly. And he invites us to seek out his Good News AND HIS HEALING GRACE.

And, let us return to our question, **"In what ways can God be the healing source of strength for us today?"**

Jesus shows us that God's love heals us from the inside out! Jesus shows us that we all matter! Jesus shows us that where there is life, there is hope!

Hope and strength for us all, to help us through those times when we are weak and weary! Hope in the healing power that comes from God!

In that, each of us is affected by one another, as we learned in our scripture today. Throughout the year, we experience dedicated service of the women here at Union who offer thanks to God for all the healing grace in our lives. There are many hours of service done on behalf of others. Our commitment indeed requires going to the source of our strength!

In that, our commitment compels us to go the extra mile to help feed our neighbors by the gifts of time and treasure month after month and year and year. We also help feed the hungry by committing to go gleaning in the nearby fields to pick vegetables for our neighbors in most need.

By our commitment to helping feed others, we not only help to heal a hurting world by our loving acts, but we also allow God to cleanse and heal our hearts so that we can do better and be better carriers of God's light in the world. Feeding our neighbors is an example of how God strengthens us to move forward by seeking God to help us root out the systemic injustices that cause so much hunger to occur, even in a wealthy nation.

And so, let us find the strength to receive God's healing power in our lives. Let us also find the strength to trust that God has given us everything we need to help us to help others. And let us continue to be the witnesses to the Good News of Jesus Christ's healing love that has come into the world! **Amen.**

PRAYER

Open our hearts to behold your glory, O God, shining in Christ, in prophets, and saints who inspire, and perhaps even shining in us. Amen.

Compassionate Community

How might we experience the glory of God today?

<u>Sunday, February 14, 2021</u>
<u>Transfiguration Sunday</u>

Compassionate Community
Today, the Gospel of Mark tells us that Jesus Christ reveals his divine identity to a small **compassionate community** within the disciples. Jesus led Peter, James, and John to a high mountain where they saw what is known as transfiguration, which was an experience that caused them to see Jesus in a new light.

And so, our question might be, **"How might we experience the glory of God today?"**

As Jesus suggests, we <u>first trust that God's presence is with us throughout life's journey and that, secondly, offers a God-like presence that shines through us and into the lives of others.</u>

But, before we go any further, how many of us remember seeing the picture of Jesus with rays of light shining around Him? Well, today's gospel passage is what inspired that glorious picture! And that is why in our Gospel story this morning, we are invited to accompany Jesus and his chosen disciples as they climb a mountain to experience a wonderful moment. As Mark 9:2, NIV reads, "Jesus took Peter, James, and John with him and led them up a high mountain, where they were all alone as it was in those moments where Jesus transfigured. In other words, Peter, James, and John would witness Jesus' appearance completely change right before their eyes - revealing that Jesus is the holy deity sent from God!

Those moments of transfiguration also included the appearance of Elijah and Moses, two of the greatest prophets in the Old Testament, which was necessary for the disciples to see. Because soon, people would say that Jesus was against the prophets. They would quickly say that Jesus had nothing to do with the prophets. But here, Elijah, Moses, and Jesus are together.

And then, in the final moments of the transfiguration, the disciples would hear the voice of God say that Jesus is His Son, that He is loved, and that they should listen to him.

And this was important for the disciples to hear. Because soon, people would say that Jesus was not the Son of God. Soon, it would seem God did not love Jesus Christ. And some religious leaders would quickly say that no one should listen to Jesus. But here, none of that is true.

God's presence was revealed high on that mountain and witnessed by the disciples, who were the beloved and compassionate community of Jesus Christ.

And, let us return to our question, **"How might we experience the glory of God today?"**

As we are blessed to experience the glory of God every time we engage in prayer, bible study, worship, and serve others because we climb the mountain with Jesus as the compassionate community to experience the glory of God revealed in Christ's love and light.

And an excellent example of life's mountaintop experience is told in a story passed along about a compassionate woman who was cheerful and optimistic even though she was ill and confined to her room, which was on a fifth-floor attic apartment, inside of an unkempt building. So, one day a friend decided to visit a sick lady and brought along another woman, who had great wealth. And since there was no elevator, the two ladies began the long climb upward.

When they reached the second floor, the well-to-do woman commented, "What a filthy place!" And her friend replied, "It's better, higher up." When they arrived on the third-floor landing, the wealthy lady remarked, "Things look even worse here." Again, her friend shared, "It's better higher up." Finally, they reached the attic level, where they found the bedridden lady, who had a smile on her face that radiated the joy that filled her heart.

And although the room in the attic was clean and flowers were on the windowsill, the wealthy visitor could not contain herself about the surroundings and blurted out, "It must be tough for you to be here, living like this!" And yet, without a moment's hesitation, the sick lady responded, "It will be better, higher up." [142] How many of us believe that it will be better higher up?

At that moment, the bedridden woman appeared to be living in a valley, but she was not looking at temporal things. Instead, her eyes of faith were on the eternal. She had surrounded herself with Jesus and His loving and compassionate community of followers. As the lady confined to her room must have seen the mountaintop experience of Christ's glory shining within her heart.

Many of our mountaintop experiences have peaks and valleys. We see this exampled by the disciples who followed Jesus up the mountain, and then, they followed Jesus when they walked down from the mountain as our life experiences have peaks and valleys.

For instance, the disciples had no idea that not long after their glorious mountaintop experience, they would soon enter a valley because things with Jesus seemed to be going so well. They witnessed Jesus perform miracles, such as miraculously walking on water and feeding the crowd of 5000. The disciples were also with large crowds, who gathered to listen to Jesus's parables. It was easy to be a disciple of Jesus during those moments. And there was no doubt, in the disciples' minds, that Jesus was the Son of God and the Savior of the world. As see that the disciples were experiencing one high point, after another, while traveling with Jesus.

But right around the corner loomed the valley as the disciples would experience the shadow of death. In that, the large crowds that gathered to witness the miracles and teachings of Jesus would soon turn against Him. Jesus would soon be betrayed, arrested, tortured, publicly condemned, and executed in one of the most shameful ways known to man.

Indeed, the valley of the shadow of death was right around the corner. And the disciples would soon be filled with fear and even doubt that Jesus was the Son of God. Soon, it would be challenging to be a disciple of Jesus Christ.

And that is why Jesus takes them to the top of a mountain. He lets the disciples experience something extraordinary with their own eyes so that they can catch a glimpse of Jesus Christ's glory and become strengthened for the valley that would soon come.

And like the disciples who witnessed a glimpse of God's glory, in our Old Testament reading, Elisha was also granted the privilege of experiencing a glimpse of God's glory. And yet, when Elijah ascends into heaven in a whirlwind, Elisha also encounters the valley of grief because he would no longer see his beloved friend. As God's love and the light were in a mighty whirlwind to two of the greatest prophets, Elijah and Elisha, to show us all that *it will be* better, higher up!

And so, as we enter the Lenten Season this Ash Wednesday, we can be like the disciples, and the prophets Elijah and Elisha, by traversing together as the compassionate community of God.

As Lent is a time for renewing our relationship with God so that we can return to the world with a renewed vitality and vision about where God is calling us to go, and we see this exampled when God called for Jesus to go into Jerusalem.

And as we travel our Lenten journey, there may be times during our 40 days and nights of Lent when it may seem at times that we are amid an uphill struggle. We remember that the invitation to climb the mountain of transformation with Jesus is always welcome.

As compassionate disciples of Christ, we must remember that we encounter God's love and light shining within our hearts. God invites us to see ourselves as a beloved community whose purpose is to shine God's light from inside our hearts and back out into the world.

Therefore, today's psalmist speaks of God's light as the rising of the sun to its setting as God shines forth and does not keep silent. And the psalmist goes on to say that God calls to the heavens above and the earth.

In other words, there is no escaping God. So, why not choose to be part of God's compassionate community, and shine forth God's love and light to everyone, everywhere? After all, the world could use more love.

And so, let us open our hearts to receive God's love, and let us shine it, everywhere, we go! May it be so. **Amen.**

CHAPTER FIVE

THE LENTEN SEASON

The Lenten Season offered some hope in the COVID-19 pandemic as more Americans would become 'fully vaccinated' and could now safely meet outdoors. This Season also faced despairing moments. Plans for stricter voting laws in various States were starting to materialize. In Atlanta, a shooter who primarily targeted Asian American women in a local spa shot and killed eight people before being apprehended. National news also reported shootings at a Dallas nightclub, a mass shooting in Colorado, and a shooting at Virginia Beach.

PRAYER

Covenanting God, help us to trust you when the evidence tells us otherwise. Help us follow you when the world says not to. Open our hearts to hear the promise of your love in our souls and live it in our world. Amen.

LETTER FORTY-SIX

God's Loving Paths

What does it mean to trust in God?

Sunday, February 21, 2021
First Sunday in Lent

God's Loving Paths

On this first Sunday of Lent, we hear that **God's loving paths** are full of signs of promise. And as we travel this Lenten journey towards Jerusalem and the cross, we are invited to trust in the signs of God's love.

And, we ask, **"What does it mean to trust in God?"**

As the scriptures tell us first to believe that God has created all things so secondly, we will always draw closer to God.

And a good example of trusting in God's loving paths is found in today's readings of Genesis. This well-known story of Noah is best known for building a large boat that he, his family, and representatives of all land animals would save from the floodwaters.

We see that God promises to protect and never destroy the earth by making a covenant with all creation. We also see that the rainbow is a sign to remind us of this promise. And, we see that God wants to be in a deep and mutual relationship with all of creation.

We also learn that the psalmist speaks of orienting oneself to God by sharing that having a deeper relationship with God requires trusting in God and relying on God's help. Depending on God's helpful and loving path is at the heart of the message for the people of faith in 1 Peter.

Peter's first letter to those early Christians clarifies the connection between the waters of the flood during the time of Noah and the baptismal waters of Jesus Christ. Peter's letter reminds us that water is a sign of God's promise and protection. And Peter also reminds us that baptism is a symbol of God's healing waters that brings forth all new beginnings.

And so, let us return to our question, **"What does it mean to trust in God?"**

As we, the beloved human creation, can respond by trusting in the healing waters of God through Jesus Christ. In that, we can trust that even through troubled waters, God's love will not let us go. We can trust that through dangerous waters, God's justice and peace keep us from falling. And we can trust that even the raging waters will not overpower the sacred water that flows that sustains our lives. In that, God's loving path leads to the healing waters that flow throughout all creation.

Jesus is a living example of how we might cleanse ourselves of whatever is troubling us to have a deeper awareness of just how deeply loved we are by a good and gracious God. And thus, reminding us of the possibilities of new beginnings unfolding in our daily living because we are all considered to be the beloved children of God.

As God tells us in the Noah story today that we are to see that the former things have come to pass and that the new things are now declared. [143] Because by faith, we will not be the same in that, we will delight in justice, and we will seek to bring forth justice to the nation. Our baptism and confirmations of faith represent the invitation into a new way of seeing how we may behave differently, seeing how we might live differently by being guided as Spirit-filled children as witnesses to Christ's power and love in the world.

This kind of divine witness speaking to God's loving paths was illustrated this past week in the PBS Special titled, 'History of the Black Church,"

[144] by Louis Gates. In viewing it, there are so many nuggets of healing and wholeness guiding a people towards love in the world. One example of God's loving presence in the PBS documentary on the Black Church was the creation of the "Freedom Singers." These singers exampled how to overcome troubling and dangerous waters with goodness. These singers included anyone who trusted in the healing waters of God. They sang in protest. They sang in praise. As the film documented, these "Freedom Singers" chanting songs like "Oh, Freedom" and "This Little Light of Mine."

As the "Freedom Singers" remind us that God's loving paths soothe our worry and fear. In that, the theology of the "Freedom Singer's" song, "Lord, Hold My Hand While I Run this Race," is another reminder that we are not alone.

Yes, humanity is still singing our "Freedom Songs" [145] because we are still in need of God's healing waters today. We need the healing waters of God to help us spiritually and emotionally with the tremendous amount of grief and loss from this past year from the impact of COVID-19. And yet, our faith calls upon us to trust and rely on God's promises because, always, God invites us into a deeper relationship.

As God's loving path is in a meaningful story passed down about a small child not even old enough for grade school, who went into one of those mirrored mazes at an amusement park.

And when her father discovered that she had slipped away, he saw her trying to find her way out and beginning to cry in fear. She became increasingly confused by all the paths until she heard her dad call out, "Don't cry, honey. Put your hands out and reach all around. You will find the door. Just follow my voice." And as he spoke, the little one became calm and found the way out soon after. And as we can all imagine, she ran into the security of her father's outstretched arms.

This is the kind of trust we are to have in God, even when life is complicated. In that, God's voice is calling us from the confusion and the maze of life. God's outstretched arms are always there, offering hope for the future so that we can keep journeying along God's loving path, which is present to guide us each step of the way.

God hears our voice, too, as God hears our cries of disappointment. God hears our cries of struggling with employment. God hears our cries of illness and our cries of grief. And, God hears our cries of repentance when we slip away.

And yet, even in these situations, we are asked to grab hold of God's outstretched arms and trust that they will always be there, even in our weakest moments, when we wonder if we can go on. Please do not give in to the troubling and raging waters and instead trust that God's healing waters will save us all. God's healing waters will wipe every tear from our eyes. Trust that God is with us. No one is alone on the path because God is with us, always.

God encourages us to stand with confidence in the face of our fears and in during chaos. And that is why we can join with the psalmist today, saying, "Make me know your ways, O God, teach me your paths." [146] As God's everlasting covenant is powerfully seen, even amid fear and chaos.

In that, love is mightier than a raging river. Love pierces the night like a bolt of lightning that gives light to the cloud-filled skies. Love rumbles over the face of the earth, shaking the ground with its message, not of fear or judgment, but grace. A baptismal message, a covenantal promise, which says, "You are my child, my beloved. With you, I am, well pleased." (Mark 1:11, NRSV)

Friends, we can genuinely believe that even in the face of fear and chaos, possibilities are unfolding because God gives us hope and reassures us of God's love through the baptismal promise of Jesus Christ, who shows us that our faith can renew us. And we can rest assured that God's healing presence is a sign, of hope, to the world, for better days ahead.

And so, let us trust in God's promise to care for all of creation. Let us also allow "Freedom Songs" to fill our hearts and heal every wounded soul. And, let us allow God's love to lead the way. May it be so. **Amen.**

PRAYER

God of peace, when the ways of this world divide us, or when we are in despair, comfort us with the power of your inclusive love, through Christ, to whom we belong and in whom we are one. **Amen.**

LETTER FORTY-SEVEN

Always Close

How might we respond to God's faithfulness today?

Always Close

On this Second Sunday in Lent, the Gospel of Mark tells us that Jesus Christ reveals to the faith community about His great suffering, death, and resurrection that is to come. As Jesus shares with the disciples that they are to follow and fully trust, God who is **always close** and is eternal, faithful.

As we might ask, **"How might we respond to God's faithfulness today?"**

In that, the scriptures suggest that believers first seek to strengthen their faith so that we will secondly trust in the promises of God.

As we hear in our scripture reading in Genesis that God makes promises with Abraham and Sarah, saying they would have children, along with having their land, and that generations will follow them.

And for those of us familiar with this story, we are aware that both, Abraham and Sarah, were of advanced age. And so, upon hearing these things, they were doubtful of fulfilling these promises from God.

And yet, God was faithful! Their names were changed, and God blessed them with a son named Isaac. Their time was not God's time. What they thought was impossible was made possible with God!

This covenantal agreement calls for Abraham and Sarah to become more faithful to God. And in faithfulness, Abraham and Sarah become mother and father of many nations as these new names become symbols and signs of new things to come.

And it is essential to note that these blessings were for Abraham and Sarah only as God has different promises of blessings for us all, and as a result, we are to wait to receive these blessings so that we can be a blessing for all of God's children.

We also see God's faithfulness with today's psalmist, as the psalmist requests help, and God responds. Once again, the faithfulness of God reveals as the psalmist praises God and invites all to join in praise.

And in Mark's gospel, the disciples are also reminded about faith and what it means to follow Jesus Christ. Jesus cautions the disciples by telling them that following Him will not be easy. [147] The disciples find it hard to believe that Jesus will suffer and die, especially since He is the Messiah!

And it is with this kind of disbelief in what Jesus shared that Peter speaks and challenges what Jesus said. And yet, Jesus responds by teaching Peter, and in effect, teaching us all that there is no benefit in gaining riches on Earth if it costs us our souls. [148]

And, let us return to our question, **"How might we respond to God's faithfulness today?"**

Well, in our response, we can seek to be faithful disciples by the trust that God's grace reaches across generations back into the past and forward into the future.

And on this last Sunday of Black History Month, it is fitting to think about the importance of reaching back to understand our present better and allow it to inform our future.

In that, it is incredible to see how God has been faithful to us through the years by showing us that if someone cuts us, we all will bleed. It is unbelievable that God faithfully shows us that we all grieve when losing a loved one. It is amazing how God's faithfulness reveals that love is universal and freely available to us all!

Being a faithful disciple is exampled in an old story about a monk. He lived in the late 4th Century. [149] As this monk made up his mind to leave the hustle and bustle of the world to live all alone in prayer along with meditating and fasting so that he could save his soul. That was his only goal. But while doing this, he later felt like something was wrong or missing from his life.

And so, one day, as he rose from his knees in prayer, it suddenly dawned on him that his life was based on a selfish, not a selfless love for God. And with this calling in his heart, the monk concluded that if he was going to serve God, he must help others. So, he said "good-bye" to the desert, and headed for the most fantastic city in the world, at the time, Rome.

Upon his arrival, the monk found that there was still an arena in Rome and still the gladiator games. Christians had to fight and kill one another, and the crowds loved it!

The popularity of these gladiator games was like watching NASCAR, the Super Bowl, or college basketball's March Madness. And so, when this monk found his way to the arena, there were thousands of people there watching.

The monk also saw the people killing each other to amuse the crowd; then, he saw the crowd's excitement as two Christians entered the area, prepared to fight. Indeed, the fight was on, and the monk was appalled!

So, he leaped over the barrier and got between the two fighters, and for a moment, they stopped fighting. However, the crowd roared, "Let the games go on." And, the two Christians pushed the monk aside. But, once again, the monk got between the fighters.

Then, the crowd threw stones at the monk, urging the fighters to kill him and get the monk out of the way. Then the commander of the games gave an order, and the gladiator's sword rose, and in that next moment, the monk was struck dead! And immediately, the crowd was silent.

They were suddenly shocked that a holy person should be in such a way. We might say they became "convicted." Because suddenly, there was a mass realization that the monk was a peacemaker through his last act of moral justice. And because of the monk's actions, the games ended abruptly that day, and they **never** began again.

As this story is like our scripture readings today, in that, the scriptures suggest our eternal life is not merely waiting for us to experience God's faithful love in the afterlife. It starts here and now. And so, we should not let life pass us by. We need to try and live it fully, with all the courage we can summon. And then, by faith, we are called to take this courage, as exampled by Jesus Christ, who led the way in showing faithful love.

Beloved, there is still a battle for moral justice among Christians today. Yet, there are also those, like that 4th-century monk standing in the middle of the battle, who faithfully seek peace.

There is a moral battle among Christians regarding how we love one another. There is a moral battle among Christians regarding equal access for all to public education, health care, affordable housing, and earning a livable wage.

Jesus Christ stands in the middle of the moral battle of loving worldly things more than we love God when Jesus teaches us that it is not okay to have an overabundance of earthly wealth and turn a blind eye to helping the poor.

Jesus Christ seeks to get in the middle of our moral battle, to bring us equal justice. In that, Jesus Christ shows inclusive love by telling us that it is not easy to follow the ways of God because, at times, it means being countercultural. It means loving our enemies. It means having the moral courage to love as God loves by putting God first, over and above the crowd's cheers, or following the divisive leaders of the day, instead of trusting in the path guided by the peaceable path of God.

As God shows us, through the peace of Jesus Christ, every moral battle, every feeling of abandonment, every cry, every prayer, and every circumstance **will** be alright! Even death cannot penetrate God's faithful promise always to be **close to us**.

In that, the storms of life, the trials, the heartaches, the disappointments are all part of the process of God stretching us, growing us, and building us into God's faithful and loving people to help guide the way of peace and justice for others so that they, too, might draw closer, to God.

And so, let us praise God for loving us from generation to generation. Let us trust in God, even in our suffering. And allow us to remain faithful disciples on the journey. **Amen.**

PRAYER

Let the words of our mouths and the meditations of our hearts be acceptable in your sight, O God, our strength and redeemer. Amen.

LETTER FORTY-EIGHT

Beautiful Law

How might we live according to God's beautiful law?

<u>Sunday, March 7, 2021</u>
Third Sunday in Lent

Beautiful Law

On this third Sunday in Lent, we learn about the importance of keeping God's **beautiful law,** which teaches those early believers how to love and care for all people.

And in knowing this, we ask, **"How might we live according to God's beautiful law?"**

The scripture suggests that we <u>first seek to live more faithfully by following God's law of love so that we can secondly faithfully live together by committing ourselves to love and care for the equal treatment of all of creation.</u>

In our Gospel lesson today, Jesus reminds the faith community about the importance of following God's law of love when He turns over the tables in the temple. And to get a better understanding of the context of this story, it is essential to know that it is nearly Passover time in Jerusalem. And that means any Jewish person who could come into town would be coming to celebrate. Jesus and His disciples are among the pilgrims who journey to

289

Jerusalem to celebrate this significant Jewish festival. And as part of the Passover, they were required to sacrifice animals.

Now, if you traveled from a long distance, odds are, you didn't bring an animal to sacrifice, you saved your money, and you would buy the right animal for the sacrifice once you arrived at Jerusalem.

So, if we are thinking with a business-type mind, we can see where this might lead. In that, there would be tons of believers coming from out of town, who need to make sacrifices, but they do not bring animals with them. Since they need to buy them from somewhere, the local believers set up places on the temple grounds to make it convenient to sell animals to these people thinking they could make a fortune by doing them a favor!

So right there in the temple courts, there were people selling oxen, sheep, and pigeons to others who needed them as a sacrifice.

And there is more. Remember, people come into Jerusalem from many places, and not everyone uses the same currency. They had their currency within the temple, so even the locals may not have had the right kind of currency on them. And since they were doing business in the temple, they needed to use temple currency. Those doing business in the temple were happy to convert other currency into temple currency for a fee, of course.

Yet, the focus is supposed to be on God, what God has done for all people, and God's ongoing presence in their midst. The reason that the people are coming into Jerusalem is to celebrate Passover. Passover is supposed to be a time for the believers to remember how God had delivered them out of bondage in Egypt, made a covenant with them, and led them into the promised land. The focus was on God and God's mighty acts to deliver all people. It was not supposed to be on the individual making profits; it was God's presence to save them through the promised Messiah.

But right there, in the temple courts, the focus has nothing to do with what God has done for people. God's house had become a place for making money, a place of buying and selling. For some, it is a place to get rich without compassion for others even though the temple courts were supposed to be a place where all could pray, where all people could be in the presence of God.

So, when Jesus sees what is happening in the temple and sees that the believers who have come to worship without enough money cannot do so, Jesus makes a whip of cords and drives out those selling the animals. Jesus also takes the moneychangers' coins, pours them out over the place, and turns over their tables.

Let us, for a moment, imagine the scene. Startled animals are going everywhere, people running this way and that, the sound of clinking coins rolling all over the temple floor! People wonder, "What is going on? Who does this guy think He is? What were we doing wrong?" And what does Jesus say as He is doing all of this?

"How dare you turn my Father's house into a market!" [150] Because that is essentially what these people have done. They have taken a place that is supposed to be aside for all people to come into God's presence and turned it into a market.

And, let us return to our question, **"How might we live according to God's beautiful law?"**

We can respond by living more faithfully, together, in how we love God, ourselves, and another. We can love in the ways of Jesus by challenging conventional thinking. Jesus shows us how the false gods of greed, pride, and unjust power structures can enter the church and adversely impact our lives.

And that is why, when Jesus went into the temple that day, it was to say that the temple was not the merchants' house. When Jesus went into the temple that day, it was to say that this was not the worshippers or the priests' house. As Jesus turns over the tables in the temple to show us that the temple is God's house, and it is to be a place of prayer, a place of worship, and the place where all people receive the loving care of God.

Jesus turns over the tables to remind the believers of God's beautiful law of love told in the Exodus story about remembering the Sabbath, which refers to having a time of rest. As keeping the Sabbath is God challenging those once enslaved in Egypt, and now wandering in the wilderness, to rest and, in effect, to take loving care of one another.

We also hear today's psalmist proclaiming God's beautiful law of love as the psalmist begins with a hymn of praise, declaring that all of creation praises God. The psalmist also shares that all people are responsible for acting in love, as revealed by God in the scriptures and the law. Then, the psalmist concludes with a prayer to God, as the creator of all, as we hear the psalmist challenging the conventional thinking of the day by joining together, both nature and humanity, in praising God!

On this Sunday, when we honor both Women's History Month and Amistad Sunday, we turn over the tables of sexism; when it enters the house of God, we turn over the tables of racism. When it enters the house of God, we turn over the tables of classism. When it enters the house of God, we turn over the tables of homophobia, when enters the house God, and we turn over the tables of any injustice when it enters the house of God by inviting all to consider a different way of faithful living.

And when thinking of faithful living, it reminds me of an old story passed about a very wealthy person in declining health, who finally gets serious about his eternal state. And so, he goes to the local pastor and asks what he can do to account for the fact that he has never given God much time, or even given the church, a dime. And the pastor looks at him with an expression that says, "Well, you finally got around to it, huh?" And with conviction, he finally says, "OK, how about if I give the church every cent I've got? Will that do it? Will that guarantee I'll go to heaven when I die if I give my entire fortune to the church?" The Pastor paused a moment, then replied, "Well, it's worth a try!"

Christ's death and resurrection are our Passover from end to eternal life. Because all the worldly stuff we acquire will only last for as long as we are in this world if even that long. Fortunes are lost. Markets go sour. Jobs are lost when companies go belly up. Droughts or floods happen, and we lose our crops for the year. We get sick. Our bodies slow down. But God is with us, with the promise of hope in the beautiful law of everlasting love, shown through Jesus Christ.

While this Gospel text may be challenging to understand when we see that Jesus gets angry and clears the temple, we can be comforted in knowing that He does it for us. He does it to remember that God calls upon us to put God first and advocate for all people no matter what, as the Season of Lent reminds us what it means for us to live faithfully together.

And so, let us continue to follow God's beautiful law of love. Let us continue to praise God above all things. And let us go out committed to turning things upside down for the well-being of our entire community. May it be so. **Amen.**

PRAYER

God, breathe upon us newness of life. Where we cannot see, help us keep our minds open toward faith. Strengthen us as we seek to know you and help us grow in love for you and each other. Amen.

No Matter What

How do we see God's love at work today?

<u>Sunday, March 14, 2021</u>
<u>Fourth Sunday in Lent</u>

No Matter What
On this fourth Sunday in Lent, we reflect upon God's love for everyone as Jesus teaches the early disciples that **no matter what**, God's love is at work in every situation of life.

And so, we ask, **"How do we see God's love, at work, today?"**

The scripture suggests that we are first to believe<u> that God's love will heal our brokenness so that we might secondly be able to offer God's love to a hurting world.</u>

And, we hear of God's love from the story that Jesus shares with the disciples. It is important to note that Jesus is speaking with Nicodemus, a religious Pharisee leader, who comes to visit Jesus in the darkness of night. Nicodemus secretly visits Jesus because he does not want to be seen by his fellow Pharisees. After all, they disagreed with Jesus and his teachings as a group. And in fact, Jesus had become very unpopular among them.

However, Nicodemus was different. He had seen or perhaps sensed something unique and special about Jesus regarding what He said and did. And as the two of them spoke that night, Nicodemus was deeply moved, as he recognizes that Jesus has the authority and guidance of God. And Nicodemus feels that the new movement around Jesus was of God.

And while Nicodemus gave reverence to Jesus, by being polite, Jesus shares the urgency of the moment. Jesus conveyed to Nicodemus that there was no time to waste. And if Nicodemus was seeking the Kingdom of God, he must make a new start.

Jesus shows this urgency by reminding Nicodemus of an event in the time of Moses, which is in today's reading on the Book of Numbers (21:6-9, NIV). Here, we hear of the hardships of the Hebrew people after escaping slavery in Egypt, during their time in the wilderness, and they began to complain. God sends fiery snakes to bite them. And the people turned to Moses for help and guidance. And he told the anxious, frightened people that he would fix a bronze replica of a serpent on a staff and that those who a snake bit should gaze up, at this, to survive the venomous bite and live.

Jesus teaches the serpent story of God at work in the Book of Numbers to help the disciples prepare for his impending death on the cross. And, just as Moses' fixed' the image of a serpent on a staff, which has often been the symbol of healing, it also is so, that Jesus would be 'fixed' upon that cross and He would die to 'heal' and restore our relationship with God. For it is written, "Just as Moses lifted up the serpent in the wilderness, so must the Son of Man be lifted up, that whoever believes in him, may have eternal life." (John 3:14, NRSV)

Now, let's return to our question, **"How do we see God's love, at work, today?"**

As we can look to the suffering of those early people of faith and see that no matter what the circumstance, God's life-giving love continues to offer healing and hope for us today.

Jesus also meets us in our difficult moments to remind us that God so loves everyone no matter what. Jesus, God's begotten Son, journeys with us so that we remain hopeful along the way, knowing that Jesus will accompany us eternally.

There is a 'tall tale' with a special meaning I like to tell about God's steadfast love at work. And we are told of someone who is unable to find their lost pet and is heartbroken. The person staples a message on a telephone phone pole to find the pet. It reads: "Lost Dog," with a description of the dog and a promise of a substantial reward to whoever found and returned the dog. And on the "Lost Dog" placard, the caption said, "He only has three legs, he is blind in the left eye, is missing his right ear, his tail is crooked, has been neutered, is almost deaf, and answers to the name, 'Lucky.'"

But obviously, the only thing that makes that dog lucky is that there is someone who loves him and wants him back. And this is the kind of steadfast love that Jesus Christ offers to us all!

It is the kind of love that keeps on giving, as the old story of the giving tree is about a tree that offers a little boy her apples to pick and her branches to climb. The boy and the tree love each other and are happy in their life together. But as the boy grows older, his interest in the tree becomes less. The tree is very lonely, but the boy returns as a young man one day. And the tree offers her apples and branches, but the boy claims that he is too old to climb and play. And he is more interested in money.

Then, he asks the tree,' Can't you give me some money?' But the tree does not have any money. However, she does have apples. So, the boy picks the apples and sells them, and he and the tree are happy. But then, the boy stays away an even longer time, and the tree is sad.

After years pass, the boy returns. And the tree is overwhelmed with joy. So, she invites the boy to swing from her branches, but the boy is too busy to play. He wants his own family and a house to keep them warm.

Then, he asks the tree to give him a house. And the tree says no but suggests that he can cut her branches and build a house with them. The boy does this, and he and the tree are happy.

Many more years passed before the boy, who had become middle-aged, would return. And the tree, overjoyed, invited him to play. But now, he is too old to play. And all he wants is a boat which will take him far away. So, he asked, 'Can you give me a boat?' And the tree invites him to cut down her trunk to make a boat so that he can be happy. Then, he cuts the tree trunk, and the tree is only somewhat satisfied because now, only a bare stump remains.

Many years would pass before his return, and he had become an older man by this time. And the tree apologizes for having nothing to offer any longer, no more apples to eat or branches to climb, only an old stump. But the older man says his teeth are too weak for apples, and he cannot climb. And that all he needs is a quiet place to sit and rest because he is exhausted.

And the tree straightened herself up as much as she could and said, 'an old stump is good for sitting and resting. Come, sit down, sit down and rest.' And so, he does, which makes the tree very happy.

The giving tree is a great concept. And yet, that apple tree is not the only one that offers life-giving love, as the Season of Lent reminds us of another life-giver. The kind of life-giver, who gave of Himself, who gave body and blood, who showed love and mercy, who gave forgiveness and compassion, who gave acquittal and freedom. Yes, the life-giver, whose name is Jesus. The One who came to give His life so that we might live life eternally.

And we know this because our gospel lesson tells us, "For God so loved the world" [151] not just one nation, but everyone, everywhere, "that he gave his only Son, that whoever believes in him should not perish, but have eternal life." Therefore, Jesus had to go on the cross.

Like the cross, the serpent is a symbol of death, which came to be a symbol of life, a symbol of giving, a symbol of sacrifice, and a symbol of true and gracious love. And we have been given this kind of love so that we can offer it to God, ourselves, and one another. And by our doing so, we can join with today's psalmist who sings about God's steadfast love restoring all who are suffering.

So, when pain and grief overwhelm when domestic and international terror and violence seem to reign when our health seems seriously compromised, and when hope seems to crumble, let us look to God's faithful, eternal love. Let us look for God to heal our broken hearts. Let us look for God to heal our troubled minds. And no matter what comes our way, let us look for God's love to bring healing, hope, and wholeness into a hurting world, now and forever. AMEN.

PRAYER

In our hearts, O God, we are known by you. Every aspect of our past and every heartbeat of our present are known and loved by you. Create in us the desire to know you, too, and in knowing you, help us live more fully as your people. Amen.

Deep in Our Hearts

How do we keep our hearts filled with Godly love?

<u>Sunday, March 21, 2021</u>
<u>Fifth Sunday in Lent</u>

Deep in Our Hearts
On this fifth Sunday in Lent, our hearts call out for God's healing, wholeness, and mercy as Jesus teaches all disciples to keep his words of love **deep in our hearts.**

And so, as we journey towards the end of this Lenten season, we ask, **"How do we keep our hearts filled with Godly love?"**

As the scripture suggests that we <u>first fill our hearts with God's spirit so that we secondly become inspired to share the love of God in the world.</u>

And today, we hear a pivotal story in John's gospel about God's love for us all as we learn that some Greeks traveled to worship God at the Jewish religious festival, which is also known as Passover. And upon entering, they request to see Jesus. And since these non-Jewish seekers had limited access to the Jewish Feast, they approached Philip, who was from Bethsaida, where many Greeks lived.

After Philip shared their request, Jesus said, "The HOUR has come for the Son of Man to be glorified." (John 12:23, NIV) In the Greek language, the word, HOUR or HORA, means "a point of time or a season when an appointed action is to begin" (Merriam Webster), which signals for us, that Jesus was looking ahead to the cross. History had been building up to this event. The one main event that he had come to earth is to be the Savior of all. By the arrival of the Greeks at Passover, it was an indication that Jews and non-Jews had come to know the glory of God. And, it was now time for the main EVENT to come to pass.

To explain why he was pleased about the Greeks at the Passover, Jesus speaks of God's love that brings everyone, Jews and non-Jews, into the harvest. Jesus explains what was about to happen at the crucifixion by giving an example of a kernel of wheat being planted in the ground and yielding a great harvest.

Jesus gives this example to get the message across to all that HE is the ONE KERNEL of wheat and that He is on His way to the cross to die, be buried, and to become resurrected so that we all might have new life. Jesus further tells them that there will be a great harvest of souls now and in future generations if He does this. And by doing so, it would not only be the fulfillment of the covenant promise for God to save the Jewish people, but it would let all know that Jesus came as the Savior of all.

Bringing us back to our question, **"How do we keep our hearts filled with Godly love?"**

Well, according to our example from today's gospel message, our hearts will remain filled with Godly love when we, like those early believers at Passover, actively desire for God to dwell, deeply, inside our hearts.

And this desire to know about God's love for us is also the message that comes to us today from the prophet Jeremiah as Jeremiah speaks of God's new covenant, which dwells within the hearts of all believers. In that, this new promise is so that all will come to know of God's forgiving love that lives deep inside our hearts.

Today's spiritual renewal message is also exampled in a story once told about a river that wanted to flow into the sea through a desert. But, when the river saw the vastness of the desert, it got afraid and said, "The desert will drink my water, and the hot breath of the sun will destroy me, and I will be reduced, to a stinking swamp." Then, the river heard a voice, saying, "Trust the desert!" But, the river questioned, "Would I still be the same? Would I lose my identity?" And the voice replied, "You can in no way remain the same!"

So, the river trusted the desert and began to flow through it. The heat of the sun turned her into vapor. It carried her into the clouds over the hot stretches of the desert. Then, formed into the rain and out of the clouds, came down a new, fresher, more beautiful river on the other side of the desert. The river became so happy that it said: "Now, I am, my real self!"

But, barrenness, dryness, or difficult times can happen to us all as they are transitional phases over to the new times of change and transformation. They are unpleasant, and they bring about fear and insecurity. And that is why people search desperately for ways and means to avoid them like the river in our story.

And yet, Jesus teaches that we should trust the desert and its dryness. Jesus is teaching we should allow change and transformation to come and reach the sea of our deepest longing so that we might grow and mature. And by our doing so, Jesus teaches us that we might one day be able to say, "Now, I am my real self!"

Jesus Christ has become a never-dying plant out of which people, of all times, draw our spiritual nourishment when facing situations that cause us to wonder how in the world we will make it through, whatever our desert experience might be, at any given moment.

Well, we just might feel God more deeply in those times of despair when we take the courage to trust the desert stages of our lives journeying into the sea of happiness towards the love of God and one another. Those of us who believe in the sea beyond the desert may not need to cling to what we have and who we are desperate for right now. Still, we can trust that we might find the shore of a new peace during the pains, insecurities, and difficulties of life, where there is happiness and community.

We see that even Jesus and His followers were not free of doubts, pain, and anxiety. We hear this when Jesus says in John 12:27, KJV, "Now my soul is troubled." And in his deep concern, He goes on to ask himself the question, "And what am I going to say, 'Father, deliver me from this hour?'" But then, He immediately answers His question, saying, "No, it is for this reason that I have come to this hour." Jesus knows that his purpose is to die as a seed for all people to have the possibility of living in faith and truth. By doing so, He will gather a great 'harvest' in His name, to the glory of God. [152]

As the way of his death was to be a way of pain and suffering, beyond imagination as Jesus was to be 'lifted up,' on a cross, for all to see. And, this would happen so that God could lift Him up out of the gloom of death into the wonder, beauty, and light of the resurrection, by opening the way for all to follow Him into life, in all its fullness.

This love for all humanity is at the heart of what Jesus teaches us today. That is why our wider church joins with other Christians, denouncing the false teachings of White Christian nationalism. It is the deep story behind the U.S. Capitol insurrection. A political vision of violence and retribution falsely teaches that God favors only a race and religious people. Jesus teaches us to love EVERYBODY as we love ourselves. In other words, God loves us equally, and we are to love each other in the same way.

And as we live through these times of false teachings of divisiveness, we can understand how Jesus and his followers became overwhelmed by the suffering and the pain of the events leading to their journey into Jerusalem. Yet, even in these moments, Jesus teaches that we do not lose sight of the love and light of God.

There is a fable about God's faithful love when things appear hopeless. And it begins by telling us that the earth was a tremendous barren plain, without a tree or plant. And an angel was sent to scatter the choicest seeds on every spot, but when Satan saw the seeds on the ground, he became determined to destroy them. So, Satan buried all the seeds in the soil and summoned sun and rain to make them rot away. With a feeling of triumph, along with a sly smile on his face, Satan took great satisfaction in his act.

Weeks later, his smile changed to scorn. The sense of triumph turned to the feeling of being beaten again. He worked so hard at burying and rotting in the ground as all those seeds. Rain and sunshine germinated and sprang up to life. Plants and flowers clothed the earth in the beauty that had been undreamt of, before." (Persian Fable, Author Unknown)

God's undying love for us all is truly amazing, and it is what today's psalmist is seeking when asking for God's forgiveness of past sins and begs for God's mercy and compassion to dwell deep inside our hearts.

For God so loved the world that he sent his only Son to form a new love relationship between God and all people. Not through the old covenant list of commandments, but a New Covenant, of grace, an offering of God's Love.

And so, let us open our hearts to draw closer to God. Let us deepen our relationship with Jesus Christ, who came to save us all with His healing, wholeness, and mercy. And let us be the good fruit of God's harvest by sharing Godly love for everyone throughout the world. May it be so. AMEN.

PRAYER

God of our salvation, we give you thanks for Jesus Christ, who remained faithful in moving forward with God's love leading the way. Help us remain faithful in our efforts to follow your loving way. Amen.

Into Jerusalem

What does it mean to celebrate Jesus?

Sunday, March 28, 2021
Sixth Sunday in Lent

Into Jerusalem
On this Palm Sunday, we are reminded of the processional parade when Jesus rides into the city of Jerusalem in peaceful protest and challenges the status quo. As the large crowd of followers celebrates His long-awaited arrival by waving branches and shouting, "Hosanna," [153] which means "save us."

And so, as we think about Jesus' entrance into Jerusalem, we can ask, **"What does it mean to celebrate Jesus?"**

As the scripture suggests, we first celebrate God's saving and liberating work, in order secondly, trust in the hope and peace found in following the ways of Jesus.

Today's story reminds us of the moment when Jesus entered Jerusalem and attracted a large crowd of people. Jesus often found himself surrounded by crowds of people. People who were for him and people who were against him. He ministered to people who discovered his ministry objectionable; people who were desperately poor and rich; people who were well in body

307

and people who were sick; those who wanted to learn from him and those who rejected his teaching.

We hear, on this day, there was an excited crowd! It was a welcoming crowd! It was a crowd that shouted in celebration! And Jesus signals to the crowd that He is Israel's Messiah and that He has come to fulfill the promise of God's presence in the world on their behalf by acknowledging their past losses. [154]

As Israel lost their land and was dominated by the Persian Empire, followed by the domination of Alexander the Great's Grecian Empire, and when Jesus entered Jerusalem, the people of Israel found themselves under the authority of the Roman Empire.

And so, with years of oppression, Israel was hoping for someone like King David to come and rescue them from the governments who ruled them. But, in their waiting, several false messiahs claimed to be God's chosen leader. And yet, when people saw Jesus heal the sick, feed the thousands, raise people from the dead, and do all kinds of miraculous works, this crowd of witnesses believed Jesus was the Messiah, who had finally come into Jerusalem.

And so, they wanted Jesus to step up his game by using all His wondrous powers to overthrow the Roman government so that the kingdom of Israel would become the powerful nation it had once been. And yet, we find that Jesus did not come to overthrow the world's governments. Instead, Jesus came to save the world in a way that no one expected.

And so, on that Palm Sunday as Jesus processes into Jerusalem, the crowd's cry of 'Hosanna,' becomes a shout of peaceful protest.

Now, let us return to our question, **"What does it mean to celebrate Jesus?"**

Well, the story of Palm Sunday teaches us to celebrate the hope for change found in the peaceful and saving actions of Jesus Christ. As we seek peace in our hearts and our world, we desire for our world to be protected from every injustice, everywhere.

Jesus was not the kind of war-driven Messiah the people in Jerusalem expected. And yet, they were right to greet Him as a king. Because His king-ship would not be one of might, it would become one of mercy. In that, He would not release the people from Roman occupation nor take revenge upon their enemies, but He would offer them redemption and forgiveness!

And this was the kind of forgiving love that today's psalmist speaks of when saying 'O God, we seek you.' [155] As we hear the psalmist give thanksgiving for God's liberating and saving work while also celebrating God's enduring love.

And today, we also hear the prophet, Isaiah, speaking about the steadfast love of God, which sustains us in times of trouble and despair. We, like the crowd of Jesus followers on that first Palm Sunday, are crying out 'Hosanna.' We seek to be saved from the false teachings of hopelessness, hatred, and divisiveness by those who claim to be Godly. We strive to move forward in uniting with the truth of God's love, justice, and peace available for all.

The saving love of God reminds me of a story told by an anonymous author. It took place in India when people traveling through the countryside discovered an injured man lying beside the road and quickly carried him to a Christian mission hospital, hoping that there would be a bed for him.

And the physician who met them at the door took one look at the injured man and immediately saw that he was an Afghan and a member of a warring tribe. And yet, the doctor said, "Bring him in; we have a bed for him."

After examining the man, the doctor found that his attacker had beaten him so severely that he had imperiled his eyesight. Without medical attention, he would have almost certainly gone blind. But rather than being grateful, the man was filled with rage.

He pleaded with the doctor to restore his sight to have retribution. As he screamed, "that he wanted revenge. And that he wanted to find the person who did that to him and retaliate." As he continued, saying, "after that, he didn't care whether he was blind the rest of his life!" But, the doctor explained to him, saying, "You're in the wrong place to talk like that, my friend, because this is a Christian hospital founded upon the teachings of Jesus Christ, who came to show us how to love and forgive one another, even our enemies."

And although the man listened, he was unmoved and responded to the doctor, saying, "Your words are meaningless to me because, in my world, revenge is the only reality that counts." Then, the doctor got up from the man's bedside, promising to return later to tell him a story about a person who once took revenge.

And as promised, later that evening, the doctor began his story by saying, 'Long ago, the British government sent a man to serve as an envoy to Afghanistan. But, on the way to his new post, he was attacked by a hostile tribe, accused of espionage, and thrown into prison with two others.

Their only comfort was a copy of a prayer book, a farewell gift given to the envoy by his sister. She wrote her name and a brief message on the inside of the cover. The book not only became a source for their prayers, but it was also a diary where they recorded their daily experiences. The envoy filled the margins of the prayer book with descriptions of both their anxieties and their faith.

And so, upon hearing of his disappearance, the envoy's family and friends back in England waited anxiously, but sadly no one ever heard from him again. Yet, somehow the prayer book survived, and twenty years later, a man browsing through a secondhand shop came across it. He located the envoy's sister whose name had been inscribed on the front of the book and sent it to her.

And with deep heartache, she read each entry. However, when she came upon the last one, she found that it was a different handwriting. It said simply that the two prisoners had been taken from their cells, publicly beaten, and then forced to dig their graves before being executed.

And at that moment, she knew what she must do. Since her brother had died a cruel death at the hands of torturers, she must repay this injustice. The doctor continued, saying, "She wanted revenge, but Christian revenge! So, she gathered all the money she could and sent it to this hospital." [156]

Her instruction was always to keep a bed free for a sick or wounded Afghan. This act was to be her revenge for her brother's torture at the hands of Afghan attackers. The wounded man was quiet, silenced by this story of such strange revenge. "My friend," the doctor whispered, "you are now lying in that same bed. Your care is her revenge."

Friends, God calls us to save one another, by the way, that we care for one another. This is love. It is the love shown to us all went Jesus went into Jerusalem. It is why the people cried 'Hosanna.'

So then, let our 'Hosanna' speak truth to power. Let our 'Hosanna' allow us to use our control for good. And, let our 'Hosanna' celebrate God's saving love, which is with us still. May it be so. **Amen.**

PRAYER

God of hope, when we are in despair, comfort us so that we may be your presence, love, and light through Christ, to whom we belong and in whom we are one. Amen.

LETTER FIFTY-TWO

It's Time to Exhale

Friday, April 2, 2021
Good Friday Ecumenical Service

It is Time to Exhale

Tonight, women ministers are making history here, in West Palm Beach! As it is with great humility that I join with each of you at the invitation of the historical Tabernacle Missionary Baptist Church in honor of the love and life of our Lord and Savior, Jesus Christ.

And as we sit at the foot of the cross tonight, let us reflect upon His last words by offering gratitude of thanks for Jesus, being our great teacher on what it means to love. In our reflection, let us give our whole selves, as an offering, for the grace and mercy granted to us through the loving sacrifice of Jesus Christ. As the abiding, inescapable, all-encompassing love of the One who is, and always shall be, the King of Kings, and Lord of Lords, the One, who paid it all. At Calvary, Jesus knew that when He stated, 'Commend my Spirit,' in Luke 23:46, NIV, it was finally time to exhale!!!

Please help me say or chat, "It is time… to exhale!"

In prayer and meditation over this last Word of Jesus, I could not help but think about the famous motion picture blockbuster, Waiting to Exhale, which featured a cast of leading ladies who would journey through life together as friends. However, throughout the storyline, they are holding their breath and waiting for those who mistreated them to love them better. But, when they stopped holding their breath, they began to accept the reality of those relationships. They began to see the love they had been waiting for was right in front of them all along. They saw the Godly love they had for one another. And then the movie ends as they finally exhaled!!

Now, let us turn to tonight's feature story, Jesus, the One who came to show us what it means to love. Jesus, the One who performed miracles. Jesus, the One who fed the multitudes. Jesus, the One who healed the sick. Jesus, the One who was a loyal friend. And yet, we see that Jesus also experienced those who rejected his love, we see that the ones who witnessed his love day after day, and cried, 'Hosanna,' as he rode into Jerusalem days later, would shout, 'Crucify him!' [157] As Jesus loved them all, they rejected His saving love. And yet, Jesus journeys onward to the cross knowing that God's love is with Him and that those who remain with him are those sent for the fulfillment of God's purpose.

The journey to the cross was not easy to travel. And yet, it reminds us that when it seems the enemy has won the battle, God says, this battle is not yours. It is mine! [158] As Jesus' example for us, God's love never fails. Even when the journey takes us to the cross and experience, those closest to us abandon us. But, in those moments, Jesus reminds us to stay near the cross. Jesus reminds us to watch and wait. Jesus reminds us to be ever trusting in God's love for us.

And this is what Jesus knew when He said, 'commend my spirit.' [159] Because at that moment, he wanted all to know that God did, what God said, God would do because, through Him, the scriptures were fulfilled. And here is the proof.

The prophet Isaiah tells us that the Lord, God, would be born of a virgin, fulfilled in Matthew's gospel. We hear that the Lord God would be the lineage of David, and it is fulfilled in Romans. We hear that the Lord, God, would be the seed of Abraham in Genesis, and again, it was fulfilled in Matthew's gospel. We hear the prophet Micah say that the Lord God would be born in Bethlehem, the same village as His birth. And we were told by the prophet Jeremiah that His birth would bring sorrow to others, and we learn of this tragic fulfillment in Matthew's gospel when Jesus had become a refugee and fled to Egypt with his parents for safety.

We see more of God's truth in the prophet, Malachi, who told us that John the Baptist would be the forerunner to the Messiah, and it came to pass. We also were told by the prophet Isaiah of the blind and sick healed, and in the gospels, we read of it happening. Next, we hear the prophet Zechariah speaking of His triumphal entry into Jerusalem, which occurred on that first Palm Sunday. And then, the prophet Isaiah tells us how He would be despised and rejected by men.

We hear more details when the psalmist speaks of Jesus' crucifixion, His drinking of wine vinegar, and the committal of His Spirit into the hands of the Father with His bones NOT broken. Then, the prophet Zechariah tells of the piercing of His side, and the prophet Isaiah even tells of His burial in a rich man's tomb, and it all comes to pass.

In all, there are more than 300 promises and more than 300 prophecies about Jesus, are fulfilled, and that is why Jesus could finally exhale on that old rugged cross and say, 'commend my spirit.' [160]

Jesus said this because He had completed this part of the journey. Luke's gospel tells us that Jesus came to save that which was lost and to example the greatest commandment, which is for us to love. And that is why we are to love like Jesus by treating everyone as our equal. We are to love like Jesus by showing kindness, even to our enemies. And we are to love like Jesus with our humility towards others and with God. And by doing these things, we will go from being lost into being found! Because when Jesus said, 'commend my spirit,' [161] it means that we are redeemed!!! It means that we are washed by the holy, precious lamb of God!!! And because of God's everlasting love shown through Jesus Christ, we can all, finally, exhale.

And for those of us who choose to trust in God's love and purpose for our lives. Please join with me in saying, 'I trust you, God. And, I am ready to exhale.' For those of us who believe that there is nothing that can separate us from the love of God. Please join me in saying, 'I trust you, God, and

Sheila Harvey

I am ready to exhale.' And so, when we trust God and exhale all the stuff that we are holding on so tightly to, we will breathe better and live life more fully.

Friends, we might be short of breath because we carry a heavy load. Whatever we are holding onto, please take a deep breath and exhale. Whatever pain, hurt, disappointment, or sorrow has our hearts heavy and wounded. Please take a deep breath and exhale. As we stand at the foot of the cross, we see that Jesus carried the cross so that we could be set free from the heaviness of this world. Jesus got up on that cross so that all would know that God so loved the world and gave his only begotten Son. so that our burdens will be light.

As we are to remember, God has journeyed with us from the beginning of time. God carried us through the times when women were property. God traveled with us when the church did not accept women into ordained Christian ministry. God journeys with us still as God has touched the heart of the pastors of Tabernacle, to have the first set of women to preach 'the seven last words of Jesus' in West Palm Beach.

The journey to equality is a long road, but it is worth taking. And it is best captured in that great Negro hymnal that says, 'Ain't Gonna Let Nobody Turn Me 'Round, I'm gonna keep on walkin', keep on talkin', walking to freedom land!!' [162] As this freedom land is the long road, to God's glory. And, when that time comes for us to take our last breath, we can say, like Jesus, 'commend my spirit.' [163] For, at this moment, we will trust that our journey was not in vain.

And so, let us inhale God's love and exhale our worries. Let us inhale God's strength and exhale our fears. And, let us inhale God's perfect peace and exhale every injustice that keeps us from trusting God's purpose for our lives. **Amen.**

316

THE CONCLUSION

Easter returns with renewed hope as millions of Covid-19 vaccine doses were given. Americans were expecting to go back to normal soon. Saint James Theatre became the first New York Broadway Theater to reopen its doors. And, Major League Baseball announced not hosting its event in Georgia after state legislators passed a voting law making it illegal to give water and food to people waiting in line to vote. [164]

PRAYER

We praise you, O God! Christ has conquered death! Make all things new in our lives on this day. Dwell in us, that we may proclaim to the world the good news of your steadfast love which endures forever. Hallelujah! Amen.

LETTER FIFTY-THREE

Now What?

Now What?

On this Resurrection Day, God reveals an astonishing revelation to the beloved disciples. The tomb is empty. JESUS CHRIST IS ALIVE! Jesus Christ has risen, as He said. As His saving love for us, through His life, death, and resurrection is indeed a reason to celebrate. But, even with renewed hope in their hearts, they still wondered, '**Now What?**'

The story of Jesus is one of hope and love. And it teaches us first to remember that despair is not the end of God's love story; and secondly, to keep resurrection hope alive in our hearts by sharing God's love with others.

In our Gospel Scripture, we see that people have varying reactions to Jesus's resurrection from the dead. We see that Mary weeps. We see that Peter runs away. And, we see that many of the other disciples have disbelief. And yet, scriptures foretold that Christ would come to heal us all. As the prophet Isaiah says, "The Spirit of the Lord GOD is upon Me Because the LORD has anointed Me to preach good tidings to the poor; He has sent Me to heal the brokenhearted. To proclaim liberty to the captives and the opening of the prison to those who are bound. To proclaim the acceptable year of the LORD, and the day of vengeance of our God; to comfort all who mourn. To give them beauty for ashes; the oil of joy for mourning; the garment of praise for the spirit of heaviness; that they may be called trees of righteousness, the planting of the LORD, that He may be glorified." (Isaiah 61:1-3 NKJV)

And, that is just what Jesus did throughout His ministry. In that, He came to heal the wounded. Jesus came to forgive the sinner. He came to advocate for the outcast. He came to speak peace to the evil-doer. And, Jesus Christ came to bring life by offering Himself as a living sacrifice so that we all might be with Him in paradise. And these beloved disciples were witnesses to these things, and they believed in Jesus Christ as the fulfillment of the promises foretold. That is why they followed Jesus Christ to the cross and even to the empty tomb.

But, when they witnessed the empty tomb, they were blown away as the women who witnessed the crucifixion of Jesus Christ on that Friday evening believed in Jesus Christ as the Messiah. But, after His crucifixion, they had to be wondering, 'Now what?' And as they pondered this question on their hearts, we can imagine that on that first Easter morning, when they saw the sun creep up slowly over the mountains and over the rolling desert hills of Palestine, they witnessed a bright morning star, symbolizing hope, that something better loomed on the horizon.

And yet, for the small group of women, who witnessed the empty tomb, hope was in short supply as their spirits were crushed by the same nails that pierced the hands and feet of Jesus. They were discouraged, disheartened, and defeated. And more than anything else, they wanted to see Jesus one last time. And to do so, they woke up early on that Resurrection morning. They wanted to honor Jesus on that Sunday morning by anointing His body with spices and perfumes, which would be like our laying flowers by the graveside.

And so, when the women arrived at an empty tomb, they were shocked that the stone was removed and stunned that Jesus' tomb was empty. As it seems that as the women pondered the question, 'Now What?' the angel reveals himself to them, during their grief, and says, "Do not be afraid."

[165] And in hearing this, we are reminded that grief comes to us all even when God's love is staring us right in the face of our hurt, our anger, and our sadness. But, even then, God's amazing love seeks to comfort us. Even today, these women example how God meets us amid our tears to comfort us in love and offer us renewed hope.

And yet, when our griefs seem like they are too much to bear, let us remember that we are not to carry it alone, just like the group of women on their way to the tomb on that Easter morning, who realized that they could not carry and move the large stone in front of the tomb on their own.

The stone itself probably weighed several hundred pounds and needed to be rolled uphill to open the tomb out of a rut in the ground. And even working together, they realized, it would be impossible for them to budge the stone, let alone move it on their own.

As this message examples to us, that by ourselves, we are not strong enough to roll our heavy stones away. And, even if we bring along our group of family and friends, we still cannot budge it, we cannot get over it, we cannot go around it, and we cannot move it, not even an inch.

That is why the scriptures tell us to celebrate God's everlasting love because God is here to help us move every stone from our lives. As we hear in today's lesson, the prophet Isaiah, speaks about how we are to celebrate God because God wipes away our tears and is bigger than death. We also hear more about celebrating God's love from today's psalmist, who gives thanks and praise for God's blessings and invites us to celebrate God's loving mercy that endures forever.

As the Good News is that the promise of God is fulfilled, and we are not alone. And, we can embrace the Risen Christ is alive in us because He is living proof that God cares about our lives and offers glimpses of hope, even in our tears. In that, the tomb is not quiet. It speaks. It proclaims! It is a promise of eternal life!

And, that is just what Jesus Christ did throughout His ministry. He came to heal the wounded. He came to forgive the sinner. He came to advocate for the outcast. He came to speak peace to the evil-doer. And, He came to bring life, by offering Himself as a living sacrifice, so that we all might be with Him, in paradise!

And that is why, today, we glorify Him, as our Lord and Savior, Jesus Christ, because he fulfilled the promises that were foretold, and He died, according to His purpose, which was to save the world from every stone.

In that, Jesus does for us what He did for Mary, for Salome, for Peter, James, and Thomas. _**He**_ rolls the stone away so that our lives will be forever changed. As we have a large stone that needs to be removed, and it is called an unclean heart. And God wants to cleanse it. God wants to purify it. God wants to remind us we are all part of the beloved community. God wants to change us from the inside out. So, that we can sing that old hymn, I KNOW I'VE BEEN CHANGED… YOU KNOW THE ANGELS IN HEAVEN, DONE SIGNED MY NAME.

Beloved, we can trust that the risen Christ is alive in us. His life, death, and resurrection are living proof that God cares about our lives. He offers us glimpses of hope even through our tears. This eternal hope is with Mary, the mother of Jesus, on that first Easter morning who, after witnessing her Son's death suddenly, on the third day, there are shouts of joy coming from the three women who just left the empty tomb as they approach her front door.

We can only imagine how it felt to hear those women who had gone with her to the cross on that Good Friday, and who now standing breathless at the door, with their eyes locked together are now, filled with resurrection joy and saying, "THE TOMB IS EMPTY, MARY! He is risen, just as He said." [166]

We can join with these early believers and celebrate that Christ is risen and death is dead! Because the tomb is broken by light! And liberty is proclaimed to the captives! The Morning Star lifts the horizon! The night is passing! Our cup overflows! And, we shall dwell, in the house of the Lord, forever!

We see God's eternal love when Jesus comes out of the tomb. It was the promise of eternal life with God!

So, let us respond to 'now what' with renewed faith, trusting peace and justice for all is possible. Let us restore our strength and confidence in the Lord, knowing that Jesus Christ lives in our hearts. Let us believe that God's hope and love conquers all because Jesus is alive! Let us be like the small group of women who, even when they were afraid, continue a faith journey towards the path that God has purposed for us all. With the belief that God can roll away every stone that hinders our faith and God's plan. So that we might be able to share with others the hope found in Jesus Christ, who came to offer us forgiveness and salvation, not for only a moment in time, but all of eternity! For Jesus Christ is Risen, He is Risen indeed! **AMEN.**

ENDNOTES

1 Axelrod, Jim, CBS Evening News, 2020. https://www.cbsnews.com/news/coronavirus-infection-outbreak-worldwide-virus-expert-warning-today-2020-03-02/
2 Chau, Nicole Brown, CBS Evening News, 2020. https://www.cbsnews.com/news/george-floyd-death-police-kimberly-gardner-st-louis/
3 Comfort, Ray. The Evidence Bible, p.435.Bridge-Logos. 2011.
4 Investor, Eugene Lang. New York Times article. Berger, 2017. https://www.nytimes.com/2017/04/08/nyregion/eugene-lang-dead-harlem-college.html
5 John 3:16, NKJV
6 John 20:21, NIV
7 John 20:21, NIV
8 Isaiah 41:10, NKJV
9 Tornado Survivors, https://www.weather.gov/safety/tornado-survivors
10 John 20:21, NIV
11 Luke 24:13-35, NIV
12 Unknown Source, Oral Story Passed Down, https://www.becquet.ca/laughter/103.htm
13 Leaning on the Everlasting Arms, Hymn based on Deuteronomy 33:27.
14 Story of the Redwood Trees, https://medium.com/@treejer/the-story-of-the-redwood-trees-ac56d4730d9e
15 Psalm 23:5, KJV
16 Acts 9:36-42, NRSV
17 2 Timothy 3:14-15, NRSV
18 Luke 18:18, NIV
19 Kuralt, Charles. On the Road with Charles Kuralt.Fawcett, 1995.
20 Unknown Source, Oral Story Passed Down, http://englishdaily626.blogspot.com/2005/12/promises.html
21 Reverend says she was among peaceful protesters tear-gassed, so Trump could "hold a Bible and look Christian"
22 Unknown Source, Oral Story Passed Down, http://franklinhillpresbyterian.org/?p=1552

23 John 3:5, NIV
24 Genesis 1:31, NIV
25 Aesop's Fables. The Oak and the Reed. Translated by George Fyler Townsend
26 Böll, Heinrich. The Stories of Heinrich Böll. McGraw-Hill Companies, 1987.
27 Matthew. 10:7, NIV
28 Leonard Louis Levinson, *Bartlett's Unfamiliar Quotations* (1972). Cited in Bill Swainson, *Encarta Book of Quotations* (2000), 624
29 Genesis 17:5, MSG
30 Cohen, Charles. The Abrahamic Religions: A Very Short Introduction. Oxford, 2020.
31 Genesis 17:7, 13 ESV
32 Psalm 86:1, ESV
33 Psalm 86:17b, NKJV
34 Matthew 10:39, MSG
35 Matthew 8:23-27, NKJV
36 Fact or Fiction. The Legend of Waldorf. Lifestyle Travel Magazine. 2014
37 Matthew 10:40, CEV
38 "Miracle of San Diego," painting, Mission Inn
39 Luke 9:48, NRSV
40 McIlroy, Andrew, An Invitation to Take a Week to Consider Jesus. Books. Google.com. 2020.
41 Unknown Source, Oral Story Passed Down, https://www.onlythebible.com/Poems/Footprints-in-the-Sand-Poem.html
42 Psalm 45:17, NIV
43 Matthew 11:28-29, NIV
44 Yancey, Philip, Soul Survivor: How Thirteen Unlikely Mentors Helped My Faith Survive the Church, p 31, WaterBrook, 2003.
45 Matthew 5:44, NIV
46 John 16:33, NASB
47 Pollock, Tim. Financial Wisdom: 9 Timeless Principles of Personal and Business Finances, p xii-xiii. Westbow Press, 2013.
48 Francis Jane Crosby, Biography, Christianity Today. https://www.christianitytoday.com/history/people/poets/fanny-crosby.html
49 Genesis 37:3, KJV
50 Matthew 15:21-28, NIV
51 Luke 23:34, NIV
52 Genesis 45:5, KJ21
53 Genesis 45:4, MSG
54 Pieta Damaged in Hammer Attack by Paul Hofmann, The New York Times, 1972.
55 Exodus 2, NIV

56 A   Mighty   Fortress   Is   Our   God,   https://www.truthmagazine.
com/a-mighty-fortress-is-our-god

57 Psalm 124:8, KJV

58 The White Flight of Derek Black. The Washington Post, article written by Eli
Saslow. 2016. https://www.washingtonpost.com/national/the-white-flight-of-
derek-black/2016/10/15/ed5f906a-8f3b-11e6-a6a3-d50061aa9fae_story.html

59 Matthew 25:21, NIV

60 Unknown Source, https://www.angelfire.com/ca5/carnyvalpearlbuttons/Kids.
html

61 Kurtz and Ketcham, Experiencing Spirituality: Finding Meaning Through
Storytelling. Tarcher Perigee, 2015.

62 Romans 12: 21, NIV

63 Star Wars is a 1977 film written and directed by George Lucas. 125 minutes

64 Romans 12: 21, NIV

65 Zondervan. 10 Minutes in the Word: Proverbs, 2018. Quote by Biblical
Commentator, William Barclay.

66 Riley, Pat, The Winner Within: A Life Plan for Team Players. Berkley. 1994.

67 Desmond Tutu, The Washington Post. Article written by Pete Early, 1986.

68 Romans 10:13, NIV

69 Matthew 20:25, NIV

70 Psalm 96:1, NIV

71 Psalm 149:4, NIV

72 Holmes, Marian Smith. The Freedom Riders, Then and Now. Smithsonian
Magazine, 2009.

73 John Lewis: Good Trouble. A Magnolia Pictures Film. Documentary, 1hr,
36min. 2020.

74 Bonhoeffer, Dietrich, Letters and Papers from Prison. Touchstone, 1997.

75 Dyck, B.G. Look Back to See Ahead, p 244. Xulon Press, 2011.

76 John 8:36, NIV

77 Must Jesus Bear the Cross Alone? Hymn written by Thomas Shepherd, 1693.

78 Romans 8:38-39, NLT

79 The Shawshank Redemption is a 1994 American drama film written and directed
by Frank Darabont and starring Tim Robbins and Morgan Freeman.

80 Limits to Diversity, based on Philippians 2:1-13. A Quaker Meeting in Eastern
Washington. Spokane, 2014.

81 Bonhoeffer, Dietrich, Letters and Papers from Prison. Touchstone, 1997.

82 Matthew 22:29, NIV

83 Exodus 20:2-17, NRSV

84 #BlackLivesMatter, BlackLivesMatter.com. 2013

85 Philippians 4:6, NLT

86 2 Corinthians 4:8a, NIV

87 Philippians 4:6-7, NKJV

88 Philippians 4:6, NRSV

89 Becoming an Anti-Racist Church. https://www.ucc.org/what-we-do/justice-local-church-ministries/justice/faithful-action-ministries/racial-justice/justice_racism_anti-racist-church/

90 Marsh, Charles. God's Long Summer: Stories of Faith and Civil Rights, Princeton University Press, 2019.

91 1 Thessalonians 1:3, NKJV

92 1 Corinthians 2:4, NIV

93 Friedberg, Albert D. Crafting the 613 Commandments: Maimonides on the Enumeration, Classification, and Formulation of the Scriptural Commandments, Academic Studies Press, 2014.

94 Matthew 5:17, NIV

95 Luke 8:31, NIV

96 "I've Been to the Mountaintop," last speech delivered by King, Memphis. 1968.

97 Deuteronomy 34:7, NIV

98 The Bill of Rights, First 10 Amendments to the U.S. Constitution

99 Mark 9:35, NIV

100 Tucker, Gregory. Word Up: Life Empowering Messages. Westbow Press, 2015.

101 Matthew 25, NRSV

102 Matthew 25:6, NASB

103 Matthew 25:1-13, NRSV

104 Joshua 24:15, ESV

105 Psalm 40:5, NIV

106 Matthew 25:27, NIV

107 McGinnis, Alan Loy. Bringing Out the Best in People. Minneapolis: Augsburg Publishing House, 1985, p. 34

108 Marsh, Charles. God's Long Summer: Stories of Faith and Civil Rights, Princeton University Press, 2019.

109 McGinnis, George. From Horizons to Space Mountain: The Life of a Disney Imagineer. Theme Park Press, 2016.

110 Psalm 123:2, ESV

111 Matthew 25:31-46, MSG

112 Matthew 22:37-39, ESV

113 May, Steve. The Story File: 1001 Contemporary Illustrations, p 145. Hendrickson, 2000.

114 Psalm 80:3, NIV

115 100 Bible Verses about God's Love for Everyone. https://www.openbible.info/topics/god_loves_everyone

116 Isaiah 40:3, NRSV

117 Isaiah 40:1, NRSV

118 History of Hymn, 'It Is Well with My Soul' https://www.umcdiscipleship.org/resources/history-of-hymns-it-is-well-with-my-soul

119 Dr. Seuss, How the Grinch Stole Christmas. Random House Children's Books. New York. 1957.

120 Psalm 126:5, NIV

121 John 1:23, NIV

122 Luke 1:26-38, NLV

123 Luke 1:26-38, NIV

124 Luke 1:37, NIV

125 Unknown Source, Oral Story Passed Down, https://www.facebook.com/731libertystreet/posts/sent-from-my-matthew-118-23-niv2011-18-this-is-how-the-birth-of-jesus-the-messia/4568815639904874/

126 Romans 8:16, KJV

127 Luke 2:13-14, NRSV

128 Isaiah 32:17-18, ERV

129 Luke 1:67-69, NRSV

130 Get Out the Vote. https://www.ucc.org/domestic-policy/ourfaithourvote_get-out-the-vote/

131 Matthew 3:2, ESV

132 Aldrich, Willard. When God Was Taken Captive: Finding Hope When Heaven Seems Silent Multnomah, 1990.

133 Psalm 29:4, NIV

134 1 Samuel 3:10-11, NRSV

135 John 13:34-35, NRSV

136 Matthew 4:19a, NIV

137 Jonah 1:2, NIV

138 Matthew 4:19, NIV

139 Mark 1:17, NIV

140 Unknown Source, Oral Story Passed Down, https://sandystrachan.wordpress.com/tag/doctor/

141 Mark 1:34, NRSV

142 Unknown Source, Oral Story Passed Down, http://albee2012.blogspot.com/2013/11/homily-2nd-sunday-of-lent-year-a.html

143 Isaiah 42:9, NRSV

144 Gates, Jr., Henry Louis. The Black Church: This Is Our Story, This Is Our Song. PBS. 2021.

145 Psalm 25:4-6, ESV

146 Songs and the Civil Rights Movement, The Martin Luther King, Jr. Research and Education Institute. Stanford.

147 Mark 8:34, ESV

148 Matthew 16:26, NIV

149 Drescher, John M. Doing What Comes Spiritually. Wipf & Stock Pub; Reissue edition (November 1, 2007)

150 John 2:16, NIV

151 John 3:16, NKJV

152 Matthew 13:30, ESV

153 Mark 11:9, NRSV

154 John 12:12-19, ESV

155 Psalm 63:1, NIV

156 Nichols, Clyde E. Lift Up Your Eyes. AuthorHouse, p 161, 2011.

157 Luke 23:21, NRSV

158 2 Chronicles 20:15, NRSV

159 Luke 23:46, NRSV

160 Luke 23:46, NRSV

161 Luke 23:46, NRSV

162 Freedom Song sung during the Civil Rights Movement to spread a message of faith.

163 Luke 23:46, KJV

164 Yes, it's illegal to give water, food to Georgia voters in line for polls. https://www.wcnc.com/article/news/verify/yes-its-illegal-to-give-water-food-to-georgia-voters-in-line-for-polls/507-88b0a0d2-0230-429e-becc-30d37565bcc9

165 Luke 2:10, NIV

166 Matthew 28:6, NIV

CPSIA information can be obtained
at www.ICGtesting.com
Printed in the USA
BVHW042132060622
639095BV00004B/26

9 781664 262850